AS GIRLS AND AS WOMEN, WE ARE MADE UP OF SO MANY DIFFERENT THINGS.

We are our DNA, and we are the hormones that course through us. We are the vitamins and minerals we eat, and we are the fears and concerns we have about what we eat. We are the insecurities we have about not looking right and the things we do to try to feel right. We are the books we read and the ones we don't want to read, too. We are the love we feel when we hug our best friend, and we are the tears we cry when someone we love won't love us back. We are grief and sadness, and we are the things we do to try and make sense of a difficult world. We are the actions we take to change the things we see that are unjust, and we are as many possibilities as there are stars in the sky.

We are bodies that work, brains that learn, hearts that love, souls that struggle and women who matter. We are strong, smart and spectacular. We don't have to be superheroes to be all of the things we want to be. We just have to be us.

OTHER BOOKS YOU MAY ENJOY

Boying Up	Mayim Bialik, PhD
HelloFlo	Naama Bloom
Hope Nation	Rose Brock
This Star Won't Go Out	Esther Earl with Lori and Wayne Earl
Rising Above: Inspiring Women in Sports	Gregory Zuckerman with Gabriel and Elijah Zuckerman

GIRLING

HOW TO BE STRONG, SMART
AND SPECTACULAR

Mayim Bialik, PhD

PENGUIN BOOKS

PENGUIN BOOKS
An imprint of Penguin Random House LLC, New York

First published in the United States of America by Philomel Books,
an imprint of Penguin Random House LLC, 2017
Published by Penguin Books, an imprint of Penguin Random House LLC, 2019

THE LIBRARY OF CONGRESS HAS CATALOGED THE PHILOMEL BOOKS EDITION AS FOLLOWS:
Names: Bialik, Mayim, author.
Title: Girling up : how to be strong, smart and spectacular / Mayim Bialik.
Description: New York, NY : Philomel Books, 2017.
Identifiers: LCCN 2016044334 | ISBN 9780399548604
Subjects: LCSH: Teenage girls—Juvenile literature. | Teenage girls—Psychology—Juvenile literature. | Adolescence—Juvenile literature.
Classification: LCC HQ798 .B53 2017 | DDC 305.235—dc23
LC record available at https://lccn.loc.gov/2016044334

Penguin Books ISBN 9780399548611

Printed in the United States of America.

10 9 8 7 6 5 4 3 2 1

Edited by Jill Santopolo.
Design by Ellice M. Lee.
Text set in Perpetua.

For my strong, smart, spectacular sons

MILES ROOSEVELT AND FREDERICK HESCHEL:

You made me a mother

and you made everything better

than the girl in me

could have ever imagined

CONTENTS

• INTRODUCTION •

*B*eing human sounds so simple. After all, we are made up of about six things: oxygen, carbon, hydrogen, nitrogen, calcium and phosphorus. These six elements make up everything that we are: the cells in our bodies and the organs in our bodies and our amazing brain, which can think and calculate and feel so many things. Just six elements can do all of that! Sounds simple, right?

Wrong! Most of the time, being human doesn't feel simple at all. We may be made up of just six things, but it usually feels like we have to manage six thousand things. And as girls becoming young women, there are so many changes that our bodies and brains and emotions go through; a lot of the time, it feels like we are being asked to handle six million things. How can a body made up of just six things make up a life that is so incredibly complicated?

Well, I had an interesting journey when I was a young woman, which I think makes me a good person to talk about the complicated parts of being alive, and in particular, about being female. You see, I was an actress starting when I was 11 years old, and I had some unexpected and unbelievably exciting success as a child and teenager. I actually had my own television show from the time I was 14 until I was 19 called *Blossom*. It was about a girl—my character!—growing up with her two brothers and her divorced dad. As an actress, I played out some of the most memorable and challenging things that happen to teenagers in front of pretty much all of America—and many other countries that aired our show as well. I experienced things like having a first kiss, buying tampons for the first time, standing up to peer pressure to drink or do drugs and forming meaningful friendships while also experiencing these things in real life. (Embarrassing but true fact: my first actual kiss was on TV!)

I took a break from my acting career when I was 19 so that I could go to college and get an undergraduate degree in neuroscience, which is the study of the brain and nervous system. After that, I studied for seven more years to get a PhD in neuroscience. That's a lot of school! I had one baby while I was in graduate school and then I had another baby after I got my PhD. Those were crazy times. Being a mom and a student meant juggling breastfeeding and changing a baby's diaper about a million times a day while going to classes, studying for exams and writing a doctoral thesis—which is basically a 300-page book—on not much sleep at all.

While I was raising my babies, I taught science to 9-to-17-year-olds and then I returned to acting, eventually landing a regular role as neurobiologist Amy Farrah Fowler on *The Big Bang Theory*. So in addition to being a scientist in real life, I play one on TV. Talk about art imitating life.

Now, you may be wondering: *What does being a child actress and then getting a PhD and having two kids and being on the number one comedy in America have to do with understanding the extra special challenges of being female?*

Well, it just so happens that being in the public eye as a child made me think a lot about the ways people look at females and what they expect of us—it's different from being a guy. I was expected to look a certain way and act a certain way—all while going from being a girl to a young woman in front of everyone's eyes. It was a lot of pressure, and it led me to realize how different the world is for women compared to men.

Studying science was something I never thought I could do, because I thought science and math were for boys. It took one special tutor when I was 15 to give me the confidence to become a scientist—but most scientists are still men, so that was hard. And dating and getting married and having babies while being a scientist was also super hard, since managing all of that in any field takes a lot of time, energy and brain power, but entering a field where women aren't always easily accepted presents its own set of challenges. That's a lot to balance.

Being an actor as an adult in a world with so much technology feels a lot like being a young person today. I may be an adult, but a lot of my personal life gets played out on social media, and it's really important to know what other people say about me, and there is a lot of pressure to look a certain way, especially because I'm female. You don't have to be a famous actor to know what that feels like!

My hope in sharing my story and my views on being female is to provide you with a sort of road map for being you. I have long felt that being female in this day and age is far more complicated than at any other time in history, and I hope that some of my experiences can be helpful. I'm a girl who didn't always fit in; I'm the girl who loved science but didn't know how to pursue it; I'm a creative person who loves the arts but also embraces a scientific perspective on life; and I am an independent woman who also loves being a mom. I've spent so much of my life challenging myself to be more and do more than I thought I could be and do, and it's paid off with a hectic and sometimes really challenging life, but it's also a life I am proud of. I want to share my passion for becoming the best woman I can be while showing you that the choices you make can and will stay with you forever in the best possible ways. You can be strong, smart and spectacular, and I hope to show you how.

I've read a lot of books in my life. Some talk about the science of the body and the brain. Some talk about the hard things about being a girl. Some talk about the amazing ways we have the ability to change the world. I want this book to be all of those things rolled into one: how to understand your body, how to love being a girl and how to become a young woman who is in charge of her decisions, confident about herself and ready to take on the world.

Let's go!

one

• HOW OUR BODIES WORK •

Welcome to *Girling Up*! Picture yourself stepping out of a sleek limousine (or SUV if that's more your style) onto a lush red carpet. There are people lining both sides of this carpet, and there is excitement in the air. The book you hold in your hands is the reason everyone is here: *Girling Up*. We are going to explore everything about being female, and the best place to start is on the inside (we'll work our way out). The body you've been given if you were born female is your ticket into this chapter, so you are already a VIP at this awesome event. We're going to talk about what makes a female body special, what changes to expect as you Girl Up and how we keep your body strong and healthy so that you have an inside-out head start on becoming strong, smart and spectacular.

From Girl to Girling Up

When girl babies and boy babies are born, they actually look a lot alike—well, except for what's below the waist—and they continue looking a lot alike for a long time after that. But there comes a time, anywhere between the ages of about 9 and 16, when puberty starts.

What exactly is puberty? Well, puberty is the time in our lives when our bodies and brains start to change. If you're female, it's the physical and chemical process of Girling Up. We start to get breasts, and our hips may get wider and more "womanly." Hair starts to grow in places where it never grew before, we may start to get pimples, and our emotions may start to feel a lot bigger than they ever did before.

For some girls, these changes happen fast. For others, they take a lot longer. Sometimes we'll start to see changes and then they may seem to stop; and some people (like me) are really late bloomers and may wonder if they are ever going to Girl Up, because it's taking so long to catch up with the other girls! There is no timetable for when it's "right" to start seeing these changes; it's kind of a waiting game.

So how does all of this happen? Do our bodies have some sort of invisible timer that starts counting down from the time we're born and when the timer goes off—*BLAM!*—we transform from a girl into a woman? Is there someone watching over us who points a giant magic finger at us when the time seems right and then we start changing? What actually happens to make our bodies change?

◆　◆　◆

XX

The easiest way to answer this question is with two Xs. That's right: what actually makes us a female is two Xs. Inside every cell in the whole body, there is something called DNA. DNA is a bunch of molecules that are packed really tightly together throughout the entire body, and DNA has all of the information that the body needs to exist. For all of us, DNA is a combination of our mom's DNA and our dad's DNA, and it has information coded in things called genes. DNA contains tens of thousands of genes, which determine physical things about us such as eye color, height and whether or not we can roll our tongue into a taco shape. (Can you? I can!) Our DNA also has genes that determine more complicated things, such as if we're the kind of person who cries at sappy movies or if we tend to be outgoing or shy.

So inside every cell, there's a compact ball of all of the information that determines pretty much everything about us. The fact that we're female is coded into our DNA. When a mom's egg cell met a dad's sperm cell and a baby started growing in her belly, the mom's and dad's DNA combined—half of his and half of hers—and it was at that very second, right when the egg and sperm met, that it was determined if each of us would be born a boy or a girl.

So what's the XX business? Well, the parts of our DNA that determine our sex kind of look like an X and a Y if you look at the DNA under a microscope. Here's a picture of X and Y *chromosomes*, the fancy word for the structure of DNA when it gets all smushed up so that it can fit inside of every cell.

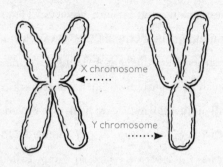

X chromosome

Y chromosome

How this all breaks down is the mom's egg cell contributes an X when her egg meets the dad's sperm. A dad's sperm cell can pass on either an X or a Y; it's basically like flipping a coin, a 50 percent chance either way. So every time a mom cell and a dad cell meet, the mom gives an X to the new baby and the dad gives either an X or a Y.

If the dad gives an X chromosome, we end up with two X chromosomes and develop into a female. If the dad gives a Y chromosome, we end up with one X chromosome and one Y chromosome, and we develop into a male. So it's actually our dads who determine if we become boys or girls. Take a second—even in your mind—right now to thank your parents for the X chromosomes! It's awesome being a girl, I promise!

Here's a simple diagram of how this X and Y stuff works.

You're probably wondering what all of these Xs and Ys have to do with how we actually start puberty. Well, the X and Y chromosomes contain chemical messages literally on the surface of their structure that get turned on at certain points in our lives. When they get turned on, they send signals through messengers in the form of proteins and chemicals to our brains. Our brains get told, "Hey! We're starting puberty here!" and the brain begins to release very special chemicals throughout our bodies. These chemicals are called hormones. Hormones are actually what makes us start puberty and are responsible for all of the changes that happen during the process of Girling Up and beyond.

Puberty and Our Bodies

Puberty changes just about every part of our bodies that we can see and even some parts we can't. In fact, scientists are still trying to fully understand how hormones affect our bodies and our brains.

Here are some of the questions I had when I started learning about puberty. Maybe you have some of these questions, too.

- What's it like to grow hair in weird places? What do I do about that?
- When are my breasts going to grow? (And why do boys look at breasts so much? Maybe I don't want that kind of attention . . .)

- What happens to boys' bodies during puberty?
- What is getting your period like? I hear it hurts and is messy.
- Doesn't your period mean you can get pregnant? How does that all work?

Let's get started by learning what happens during puberty for everybody. Both boys and girls will start to get hair under their arms, although boys tend to end up with more underarm hair than girls in general. Girls will start to get hair growing on their labia, which is the outermost part of the external genitalia, and boys start growing hair around their penis. Boys and girls both have a growth spurt at puberty, although boys' growth spurts tend to happen later, which means girls are generally taller than boys for a few awkward years at school dances!

A couple of changes that happen to boys that don't typically happen for girls is that boys' voices start to get deeper and their shoulders broaden. This is due to a special hormone they make a lot more of than we do called testosterone.

Hair

While it is generally accepted that women shave their legs and underarms and men don't, for almost all of human history, in most places in the world, women did not shave. Hair does not make you sweat more, and underarm odor actually comes from the combination of sweat and the bacteria that live on hair and in the clothing that touches your underarms rather than from the hair itself. Shaving is something that is a very personal decision, and there is nothing wrong with waiting to start shaving or not shaving at all. Trends shift, and there are many men who now like to shave their bodies. It's totally up to you, but know that once you start shaving, you will need to keep it up if you want to continue to not have hair in those places. There are longer-lasting methods, like waxing and laser hair removal, that can keep hair from growing back for longer periods of time so you don't need to keep shaving, but if you are a "low-maintenance" female like I am, you may decide that that's all too much work, and that's fine too!

What Are the Things Specific to Being Female That Happen During Puberty?

CHANGES TO BREASTS

The upper half of the female body changes during puberty with the development of breasts. Everybody's breasts develop differently, and there is no right or wrong way for them to grow. For some girls, breasts start to grow slowly, and it can take a few years to arrive at what their final breast size turns out to be. For other girls, their breast size seems to change really quickly, and they might get stretch marks along their breasts if the changes happen too fast for their body to keep up with. These marks fade with age and usually they are hardly noticeable by the time puberty ends.

Breasts actually vary a lot, even though the images of breasts we tend to see in the media show a certain shape and size that's generally thought of as "normal." Some breasts are round; others aren't as round. Some seem to stand up, while others hang down more. Here's an interesting fact: most girls have breasts that are actually different sizes, but very slightly. There are some people whose breasts are more noticeably different—one breast may even be a cup size bigger than the other.

There are different types of nipples, too. Some people have larger nipples or smaller nipples, and the dark skin around the nipple—the areola—can also vary in size. Some people even have nipples that seem to tuck in partially or completely. These are called pseudo-inverted or inverted nipples, and if you have one or even two like this, don't worry. They tend to run in families, and as you get older, they will be less noticeably different. (And if you choose to have babies when you grow up, know that you can breastfeed even with nipples like this!)

Here are some sketches of different kinds of breasts. They may look different, but remember, all of these are normal!

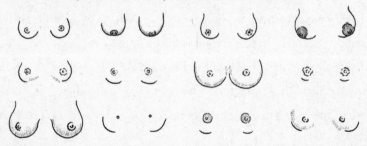

What size breasts you end up with and when they start to develop is mostly due to genetic factors, and while it's often true that your body will be similar to your mom's, it's not always the case. I was a really late bloomer, and people teased me a lot for being "flat-chested" until I was about 16 or 17. It hurt to be teased, especially because wherever I looked—on TV, in magazines, on billboards—breasts were everywhere and it seemed like people placed a lot of importance on them. I obviously eventually grew breasts just like everybody else and happened to have more of my grandmother's genetics in the breasts department than my mom's! It was hard being the last girl in my class to need a bra, but now that I look back on it, I wish I had been able to say to all of the people who teased me for being a late bloomer, "So what?!"

Does Size Matter?

There's a lot of talk in our culture about breasts, and a lot of attention is paid to who has the biggest breasts. Especially in the teen years, boys tend to be very interested in girls with large breasts, and because they have not matured enough to know to not stare and point and be kind of annoying about it, it can be really . . . well, annoying. But it's not completely their fault; it's kind of biology. Boys tend to be really fascinated with breasts because breasts are sexual organs in addition to being the things mammals use to feed our babies. For all of mammalian history, our brains have been wired to see breasts as things that represent and stimulate arousal. Breasts are sensitive to touch, and they are a very accessible part of our sexual bodies because they are just right there in plain view. The simple science is that boys get a really good feeling in their bodies when they see breasts, and until they mature a bit, it can seem like it's all they think about. And big breasts simply get more notice because they are easier to spot. But did you know that there have been times in history when having small breasts was considered more attractive? Yup! In the 1920s in America, for example, women who were busty would "bind" their breasts so they didn't look like they were voluptuous! So keep that in mind if you feel you don't like the size of your breasts—who knows what will be in fashion in a few years! Also, it's important to know that once boys become men and once you start dating more seriously, you'll learn that there is a lot of variation regarding what bodies people find attractive. Some people like small breasts, and some like bigger breasts, so don't worry that your breast size might make you unattractive once puberty is over. Your body is beautiful, no matter the size of your breasts!

CHANGES AHEAD!

The lower half of the female body looks pretty simple from the outside. That's because all you see is the vagina, and mostly it's known for being the thing that we pee out of. But that's actually not true:

we pee out of a long tube called the urethra that leads from the bladder—where pee is stored—to an opening that is really close to the front of the vagina. So there are actually two openings of this part of your body: the vagina itself, which leads from where a baby grows to the outside of your body, and the urethra. In addition, there is a very important part of your external genitalia called the clitoris, which is about the size of a pea. It is made of a smooth muscle, so sometimes it feels kind of spongy and other times it can feel more firm. It's super important, because it has about 8,000 nerve endings, making it the most sensitive part of your body.

Self-Discovery

Puberty is a time when both boys and girls show an increased interest in their bodies, especially the parts that feel good when they're touched in certain ways. When you touch yourself, it's called masturbation. While some cultures and religions have strong opinions about masturbation not being healthy or good for you, it is widely accepted that there is nothing wrong with touching yourself; your body was designed with parts that feel good when you touch them, and that's very important! At different times in your life, you may have more or less interest in masturbating, but pretty much everyone does it and it's totally okay to learn about your body in this way.

Here's a little sketch of your external genitalia.

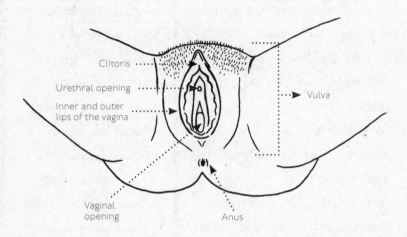

Clitoris ......

Urethral opening ......

Inner and outer
lips of the vagina ......

Vulva

Vaginal
opening

Anus

All of the workings of the female reproductive system are tucked up inside of our bodies. The vagina is sort of a passageway that leads to a really important and amazing part of you called the uterus. The uterus is where babies grow, and when a baby is born, it moves from the uterus and comes out of the vagina. On either side of the uterus, right below where the belly button is, there is a set of organs called ovaries. Each ovary is about the size of an almond, and they are where your egg cells are stored from before the time you are even born. Egg cells from the ovaries are needed to make a baby, and they are what will be involved in the most notable developments in puberty.

Here is a basic diagram of the female body showing the vagina, uterus and ovaries.

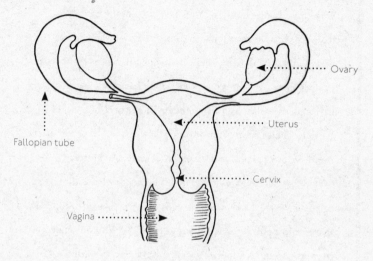

Ovary

Uterus

Fallopian tube

Cervix

Vagina

Here is a basic diagram of the male body.

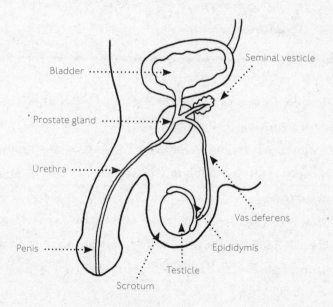

Bladder

Seminal vesticle

Prostate gland

Urethra

Vas deferens

Penis

Epididymis

Testicle

Scrotum

Boys' Bodies

Even though we're talking about girls, it's important to know what boys' bodies look like, too. The parts of the male and female anatomies are similar in some ways even though our bodies look so different. There are many differences that become evident as we grow. Boys obviously don't have a vagina; they have a penis, which leads from the inside of their body to the outside. Their urethra runs through the center of the penis and they have one opening, not two like we have. And instead of ovaries, which we have tucked up inside of our bodies to store egg cells, boys have their sperm cells housed in a pair of testicles that rest in a pouch called the scrotum. The scrotum is under the penis on the outside of the body, and it is very sensitive. (If you've ever seen a guy get hit in the testicles, you can tell it is very painful!) Sperm cells are needed if, once the boy becomes a man, he wants to have children.

How do the ovaries react to the signals of puberty? Well, the hormonal signals our body sends out when we start puberty tell the ovaries to start releasing egg cells. The egg cell is sent into a sort of hallway called a fallopian tube that connects the ovary to the uterus.

Now, before you scream, "I'm not ready to have a baby!" trust me: I know! But here's the deal: puberty is the human body's way of getting ready for the day in the future when you might want to have a baby, and puberty means it starts preparing right now.

An egg cell in the uterus has two fates: If it meets with a sperm cell, it can become fertilized and develop into a baby. If it doesn't meet with a sperm cell, it won't become fertilized and can't develop into a baby. Each month, the body prepares for the release of an egg from the ovaries by making the uterus ready for a fertilized egg by increasing tissue lining the uterus (and doing some other things too). When an egg has not been fertilized, the body gets rid of the tissue lining along with some blood. This is called menstruation.

MENSTRUATION

The hormones of the female body generally cause an egg to be released from one of the ovaries once a month or so, with the ovaries taking turns month to month. The egg cell is actually super teeny tiny, even smaller than the "." on this letter i.

Every 28 days or so, for about 4 to 7 days, you will experience menstruation, which is more commonly called "having your period" (or some people call it "getting a visit from Aunt Flow"). Not a lot of blood comes out of you every time you get your period; it's actually a total of less than a quarter cup, but it's enough so that you will need to use either sanitary napkins (pads) or tampons to catch the blood. Some days of your period, you will have a heavier flow, and other days it may not seem like much blood at all. It's a good idea to be aware of what your body typically does during your period so you can know if anything seems different or needs attention. Often the first person to know that something's not quite right with your body is you—so pay attention, and if something seems different or feels wrong, you can talk to a doctor or trusted grown-up about it. It's empowering to be able to take care of yourself in that way.

Choosing pads or tampons or another kind of menstrual product is a decision every girl will have to make for herself. Personally, I didn't use tampons until a few years after I got my period, and I never really liked them that much. There are lots of rumors about tampons, including that you can only use them if you have had sex before. That's not true! Even if you have never had sex, you can use a tampon, and it won't affect the part of your body that is affected by sex. When you put a tampon in, you have to RELAX your body and breathe slowly so you don't tense up, which can make the muscles of your vagina push it out. Even though it might sound strange, putting a foot up on the edge of the bathtub is the easiest way to try and use a tampon. (That's one of the tampon rumors that's true.) Tampons have been linked to toxic shock syndrome, a very rare but dangerous infection, so if you sleep with a tampon in, change it after 8 hours, and change it after 6 hours in the day.

There are other ways to manage your period, such as silicone cups and natural sponges, and some women even use pads that can be washed and dried and used every month again and again to cut back on environmental waste! You'll find what works best for you.

Make sure to always carry something with you in case your period sneaks up on you! When you first start getting your period, it may not be entirely regular, and that's okay. You may skip a month or two until the hormones of your body even out a bit. You should talk to your doctor about when you start and make sure everything is progressing okay as you go on. Usually, a mom or another person close to you can help you know what's to be expected.

Patterns of Your Period?

While most women have a period every 28 days or so, many girls have cycles of different lengths, and it doesn't always mean there's something wrong. Some girls have a shorter cycle, especially as they start menstruation, and some will have an even longer cycle. Charting your cycle is very important for your knowledge of your body and your health, because sometimes certain patterns can indicate something that needs further attention. Speaking to your doctor about how often you get your period will help your doctor determine if more information is needed about your cycle. I use a chart like this:

	Jan	Feb	Mar	Apr	May	Jun	Jul	Aug	Sep	Oct	Nov	Dec
1												
2												
3												
4												
5				●								
6												
7		●	●									
8												
9				⊥								
10	●											
11		⊥										
12			⊥									
13												
14	⊥											
15												
16												
17												
18												
19												
20												
21												
22												
23												
24												
25												
26												
27												
28												
29		■										
30		■										
31		■		■		■			■		■	

There are also apps for your phone to help you chart your cycle if you prefer that. Sometimes young girls are told to go on pills to make their periods more regular before their bodies even have time to figure it out without pills. It's important to know your body's schedule so that you can be in charge of it!

Here is a diagram of what happens during your period.

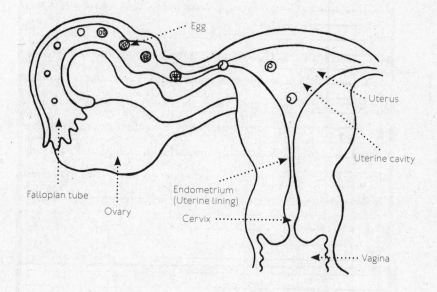

Sometimes your body can feel tense or sore or achy before or during your period. Having pain and a cramping feeling in your stomach—actually, just below your stomach, which is where your uterus is!—is caused by the uterus working to push out the lining that has been building up with blood over the past weeks in preparation to make a home for a fertilized egg. Every body is different, and while some mild to medium discomfort is fairly normal during your period, some people experience more intense cramping. The day or two before your period and the first day or two that it's happening are usually the most intense. Taking it easy as much as possible during your period, using a hot water bottle for your stomach and avoiding caffeine such as in coffee and soda can make the cramps better, and sometimes taking a short walk can relieve the discomfort. Certain yoga positions can help cramps feel less painful, particularly poses that increase blood flow to your belly in helpful ways, such as squatting positions, arching poses and resting poses like child's pose. There are medications you can take to ease the discomfort, such as those with ibuprofen, but some medicines have side effects for younger bodies, so you should consult with a trusted grown-up before trying those. If the cramps and pain prevent you from getting out of bed or hurt so much they make you throw up, definitely talk to a parent, a teacher or nurse at school or your family doctor.

Yoga Poses for Cramps

The key for all of these poses is to hold them as long as is comfortable without straining or feeling super icky. Aim for holding them anywhere from 30 seconds to one minute, but it's totally okay to start with 15 seconds if that's all that feels doable! Breathing deeply and slowly and imagining the breath loosening up all of the places that feel cramped in your belly is really important for releasing the tension you are holding there.

1. Squatting pose
2. Camel pose
3. Child's pose
4. Arching pigeon

Another thing that can happen when you get your period is that your mood can change. This is because what happens during puberty is due to changes in the chemicals released from your brain. In the week leading up to your period, there's a big shift in two very special chemicals called estrogen and progesterone. The shifts in these hormones can cause some people to feel sad, angry, frustrated or just plain old down in the dumps. (Some of us get migraines around the time of our period, which is a real drag!) Changes in mood typically pass once your period starts, and some of the same things that I recommended to ease menstrual cramps can also help your mood feel better, such as resting, getting some light exercise or stretching. If you experience a lot of upset feelings and find yourself crying a lot around the time of your period, or if you feel so sad that it's hard to get out of bed and participate in activities you usually like, talk to your doctor or a grown-up you trust.

BEHAVIOR

Hormones do so many things during puberty: they change the way we look, and they make our bodies grow and do all sorts of new things. One of the main things that hormones do for us during puberty is they change our behavior. We may start acting differently and taking interest in things in a different way—we might start thinking about dating or wondering a lot about how other people see us and if they like us and find us attractive—and it's all because of hormones. The puberty hormones are getting us ready to be grown-ups and eventually parents if we choose that path. And even if you're not ready now, it's important to understand what role hormones are playing in starting the process of turning you into an adult.

How we behave is generally different because some of us have two X chromosomes and some of us have an X and a Y chromosome; it's the basis for people saying things like "boys and girls are so different!" Let me explain a little more. Girls have a certain set of DNA that is programmed to make us generally behave in certain ways. And boys have a different set of DNA that makes them generally behave in certain other ways. You may have heard the word *feminine* used to describe traditionally female behaviors and the word *masculine* used to describe traditionally male behaviors. These words don't always apply to every girl or boy you know, but I'm sure you can think of examples from your own life of feminine and masculine behaviors and characteristics. Here are some common stereotypes that we often hear about boys and girls, which relate to feminine and masculine qualities.

FEMININE	MASCULINE
Girls like to dress up and put on makeup	Boys like cars and wrestling and making jokes about body functions
Girls spend a lot of time talking on the phone and texting their friends	Boys aren't good communicators
Girls are romantic	Boys like rough sports
Girls are very emotional	Boys tend to be pretty unemotional

Here's something interesting to know: there are certain things about boys and girls that tend to be true in all different parts of the world. For example, girls tend to talk more than boys, and that is pretty much true everywhere in the world. Does that mean that every single girl talks more than every single boy? Of course not. It just means that in general, certain things about girls and boys are true.

Look at the chart again. Do any of these descriptions sound wrong? Or do they not match someone you know? For example, do you know any boys who like to dress up and are kind of emotional?

I sure do. Do you know any girls who love cars and like things that other people say are "boy things"? I'm sure you do.

When I was young, I liked a lot of things that people said were for boys. I liked rough sports, and I didn't understand why a lot of girls wanted to talk on the phone about all of the boys in our class. You see, I was not a very "feminine" girl.

As an adult, I like a lot of things that people say are traditionally for guys, and I don't like many things that people say women are "supposed to" like. For example, I don't really like dressing up, and I don't like putting on makeup or getting my nails done. I like superhero and action movies, and I could sit and watch football all day long if you let me. I get chills when I see a Ferrari drive by. So I'm not a very "feminine" woman. And that's okay.

Even though DNA determines whether we have a vagina or a penis, and even though DNA generally guides how we behave, there is a lot of variation in how people act and feel, and that doesn't mean there is something wrong with them. There are girls who are feminine and girls who are not as feminine, and there are boys who are masculine and boys who are not as masculine. The things we think are feminine or masculine in our culture may not be considered the same in other cultures; that's how variable these things can be.

A lot of times, girls who are not feminine and boys who are not masculine get teased for being different. This can be really painful for them. It is important to understand that there are all different kinds of people and there is nothing wrong with liking what you like and being who you are. There are some places in the world where being different in this way is seen as a bad thing. In some cultures, people can be described as masculine, feminine or another category of gender that has qualities of both masculine and feminine. In fact, descriptions of more than two genders have been recorded for thousands of years.

There has been a lot of discussion in the United States and some other countries in the past few years about people who feel that even though their DNA says that they are female, they don't feel female, or even if their DNA says that they are male, they don't feel male. These people are what's called transgender. Some transgender people want their external appearance to match their internal feelings, and others don't. There's not a right or a wrong answer to what to do in that situation and there is nothing bad or wrong about people being this way.

What is important to acknowledge is that not everybody's body works the same as anyone else's, and no one knows what is going on in someone else's brain and heart unless they are that person. There has been some amazing scientific research looking at the hormone levels in the brains and bodies of people who say they feel like they don't match their DNA. Research is indicating that there are real hormonal differences, and my hope is that we can find a way for all people to feel welcome living however they feel the most comfortable.

◆　◆　◆

Wrapping Up

We've talked about some big stuff in this chapter, haven't we? We've talked about the changes our bodies go through in the process of going from being a girl to being a young woman to eventually becoming a full-on grown-up woman. We've also talked about how the changes in our bodies can sometimes feel hard to manage, and how a lot of girls feel like they can't live up to what we see as "normal," even though most of us are well within the range of normal!

You may have a mom or dad who's totally cool with talking to you about the changes in your body and how it affects you, but a lot of times, it can be hard to talk about this stuff with your parents or even with your older siblings or friends. It can feel lonely, and I remember having a lot of questions no one knew to try to answer because I was too afraid to ask them. I hope this chapter has helped answer some questions, and maybe it's given you some new vocabulary and some understanding of what the questions are so that you can start asking them whenever you're ready.

· HOW WE GROW ·

Now that we've talked about how a body gets to be female and how puberty changes you from a girl to a woman, let's talk about what our bodies need to stay strong. Does it matter what kinds of foods we eat? (Yes!) Does it matter what kind of decisions we make about how we treat our bodies? (Yes!) I actually wrote a book a few years ago with our family pediatrician about the science of nutrition and diet choices and the importance of putting a lot of thought into how we feed our bodies. I know I want to be well informed about what I eat—and enjoy the food I eat, too!—and it's very important to understand how our bodies use the fuel we give them when we eat and drink.

Drink Up!

Let's start with the basics. Remember how we're made of a bunch of molecules? Well, it turns out that all of those molecules combine in such a way that we are basically made of water. That's right!

About 60 percent of our bodies are made up of water. If the amount of water in our bodies changes because we don't drink enough—or even too much—we can feel really gross, and we can get pretty sick. What this means is that the body needs to be hydrated in a very special way. There are minerals called electrolytes in blood, urine and all of the fluid in the body. We take them in from the foods we eat and the beverages we drink. Examples of electrolytes are sodium, potassium and calcium. The thing about electrolytes is that they carry an electric charge; some are positively charged, and some are negatively charged—think of them like batteries with a positive or negative end. We have to have the right amount of electrolyte charges for our bodies to function properly.

So the first important thing to know about nutrition and how to feed your body is that it needs tons of water. Now, I'm not going to pretend like I'm the kind of person who never drinks soda or juice or anything like that. But I will tell you that most people don't drink as much water as they should, and we should all try and aim for drinking as many ounces as half of our body weight per day. So if you weigh 100 pounds, aim for 50 ounces of water, for example.

And what's wrong with soda and juice? Well, they taste good because they are full of sugar, and sugar tastes great. But the problem with sugar is that it kind of messes with the chemistry of the body and can make us feel moody and jittery. Sometimes if you eat or drink too much sugar, it can make your stomach feel queasy. Sugar is bad for teeth because it's the favorite food of the bacteria that live in our mouths that eventually wear away the protective enamel layer of our teeth, which can give us cavities. Too much sugar can weaken our immune system, which makes us less likely to be able to fight off things like colds or the flu. Also, sugar has addictive properties. What this means is that sugar gets into the cells of the body in such a way that when it doesn't have sugar, it makes us feel like we really need it. Not having sugar when our body is addicted to it makes us feel grumpy and shaky and really out of sorts. The more sugar we have, the more chances we have that our body will get addicted, so cutting back on sugary drinks is a great thing to start considering for your overall health.

Here are some of the things that can happen to you and your body if you get dehydrated because you haven't had enough water:

- dry lips and mouth
- cracking skin
- not sleeping well
- feeling tired all day
- getting sick a lot
- having a hard time concentrating
- muscle cramps
- headaches
- dizziness
- bad breath
- not being able to poop (!)

None of those things are fun!

Water World Experiment

Drinking only water every day all day sounds awful; I know. But maybe it's worth trying as an experiment—even for a few weeks. Here's what I do to make water more fun: I add sliced oranges or cucumbers or even strawberries to plain water so it tastes a little more interesting. And then I save soda and juice for special occasions. Part of getting into the habit of drinking more water than soda or juice is to give your body a few weeks to adjust; it takes about that amount of time to let your body lose the craving for sugary drinks. If you do a two-week experiment and add to your experiment cutting back on other high-sugar treats, I bet you'll be amazed at the shift in your taste buds!

Eat Up!

All right, what are some of the basic things our bodies need in terms of food? The government recommends that meals in the United States should include foods from the following categories: fruits and vegetables, protein, grains, and dairy (or a nondairy source of calcium if you choose to stay away from dairy). Here are the basics of what you need to know about all of the things there are to eat.

FRUITS & VEGETABLES

Has anyone ever told you how important it is to eat your vegetables? Well, I hate to say it, but they were right. Same goes for fruits. Fruits and vegetables are super important. They contain vitamins and minerals such as potassium, fiber, thiamin, niacin, folate (folic acid) and vitamins A, B, C, D and K. The body takes all of these in and uses them to do things like make hair strong, keep nails healthy, keep skin looking pretty and keep the brain working well so we can both listen in class and have a lot of leftover energy after school to hang out and play games and talk to friends. Vitamins and minerals do so many things in the body, and without them, we'd really be in bad shape. So please: eat your vegetables—and your fruits!

Fruits and vege-
tables are especially
important to eat in as
natural a form as possi-
ble. Meaning: however
the fruit or vegetable
grows is probably the
healthiest way to eat it,

and if it needs cooking, the less you add to it, the better. So instead of dredging strawberries in maple syrup and covering them with powdered sugar, learn to love strawberries exactly as they are! And think about a sweet potato. The healthiest way to eat it is baked, not mixed with marshmallows and sugar and butter and made into a sweet potato casserole—although if you're going to eat it that way, once a year on Thanksgiving is a good time to do that! With a few exceptions (such as carrots, tomatoes and egg-plant, which actually increase in nutritional value when you cook them a little bit), pretty much every fruit and vegetable is healthier to eat just the way it grows or with only slight cooking and very little sauce on it.

PROTEIN

When you think of protein, you probably think of the most common way people in the United States eat protein: by eating meat. Chicken, beef, pork, lamb and fish are the most commonly known sources of protein in this country. Protein is what all of the cells are made of in every single part of the body and brain. And protein itself is made up of twenty amino acids, nine of which the body cannot produce on its own, which are called essential amino acids because they are . . . well, essential. In order for the body to support the brain, spinal cord, digestive system, kidneys and immune system properly, we need to eat things with plenty of protein to get all of those amino acids. Without the correct amount of protein, our muscles won't work, our cells can't be properly repaired if they get hurt by toxins in the body and environment, and we can't even think straight. (Interestingly, too much protein can cause health problems too, so it's important to know how much you actually need.)

While in our country eating animal protein is very common, there are many healthy countries around the world where people don't get all of their protein from animals; they get it from non-animal sources such as beans, nuts and seeds. You can also find protein in things like rice and even bread and pasta. People who don't eat meat for health reasons or because they don't like the idea of animals being used for food can still get the right amount of protein.

And although there has been a trend of young girls in particular adopting a vegetarian or vegan diet as a way to lose weight, avoiding or limiting the animal products you consume is a lifestyle choice that should be done with care and conscious decision-making; it's not a way to lose weight. If you think choosing a restricted diet is a solution to your body image or weight concerns, talk to a health care provider or counselor, because you may benefit from a closer look at your relationship to food and your body.

Where's the Beef?

Meat, cheese and fish are not the only ways to get protein! Here are some of my favorite ways to get protein without using animal sources.

- **Beans:** Three-bean chili is one of my favorite ways to get a high-protein meal. Adding beans to burritos, salads and even pastas is an easy, yummy way to get plenty of protein. And beans are delicious when they're turned into spreads like hummus, so keep an open mind about beans; you'd be surprised what they can do for your taste buds and your protein intake.
- **Soy:** While soy products should be eaten in moderation, tofu (mildly processed soy beans) is a great protein source

and can be added to stir-fries and salads with minimal food preparation needed. Processed soy is available in ground form for use in tacos and burritos, and there are many ways soy beans make for great protein sources in ways you never imagined, such as in veggie burgers and even cheese slices.

- **Nuts:** You might like peanut butter (I sure do!), but have you ever tried almond butter? It's just as yummy and has more "good" fats (the monounsaturated kind) and less of the "bad" fats (the saturated kind). Learning to love snacking on raw almonds, walnuts and cashews is a terrific way to get protein and also healthy fats. A handful of almonds and an apple is one of my favorite snacks.

- **Other choices:** Grains like oats and quinoa, which is actually a seed, have a ton of protein.

CARBOHYDRATES

Carbohydrates are the main source of energy for our bodies, and when we eat carbohydrates, they are broken down into sugars—a good kind. Carbohydrates are important because they are built of sugar. And I know we just talked about how a lot of sugar isn't good for us, but the right kinds of sugar—such as those found in healthy carb-heavy foods—are super important for giving our bodies energy. What powers our bodies and our brains is carbohydrates! Whether you are going to do sit-ups in gym class or cram for your algebra test, your body needs carbs to get your muscles moving efficiently and your brain thinking clearly. Have you ever heard anyone say that breakfast is the most important meal of the day? That's because overnight, when you aren't eating or drinking anything, the level of sugars in your body drops and in the morning, eating carbohydrates helps jump-start the brain and the body. Carbohydrates generally come from starchy foods like rice, oats, bread and pasta. They can also be found in certain fruits and vegetables such as bananas, broccoli, carrots, apples and potatoes.

Sometimes we hear people saying that they want to "cut back on carbs" and that carbohydrates are bad for us. It actually turns out that carbohydrates themselves are good for us, but the way we eat them tends to be with a lot of sauce and often a lot of added artificial sugar and fat. So for example, pasta can be a great healthy meal that provides a lot of long-term energy (runners tend to eat pasta before they do a big marathon!), but if you throw a ton of cheese and butter on the pasta, it can actually make your energy *decrease*. And if we don't move our bodies enough, carbs don't get burned off, which can contribute to weight gain. Foods made with whole grains, like whole-wheat bread and whole-wheat pasta, are broken down by the body slower, so you feel fuller for longer, meaning whole grains provide a better source of energy for your body.

Gluten is a protein found in any food made with wheat, barley or rye, which are in a lot of the most common carbohydrate products like bread and pasta. Some people are allergic to gluten and they don't feel well when they eat it. People with celiac disease aren't able to digest gluten at all, and it can be dangerous for them to eat even a little bit of something containing gluten. If you notice that you get gassy, bloated or constipated after eating bread or pasta, talk to your doctor about it. There are lots of gluten-free bread and pasta choices around that are really delicious, so don't worry if you need to limit your gluten intake.

DAIRY OR NONDAIRY CALCIUM

A small portion of the government's recommendation of what we should eat is dedicated to dairy or to a nondairy source of calcium. Dairy is high in calcium and protein, but it can also be high in fat and sugar and salt, so you want to be careful which dairy you choose to eat. For example, eating yogurt for breakfast is very different from eating a giant ice cream sundae every day as your source of dairy. A lot of people get an upset stomach when they eat dairy because most of the population actually can't fully break down the milk protein from cow's milk. Up to 95 percent of certain groups of people such as African Americans, Asian Americans, Jewish people of Eastern European descent and Native Americans can't process dairy well at all. If you've ever noticed that you get a gross feeling in your stomach after eating pizza or ice cream, speak to your parent or even the school nurse about it. There are plenty of ways to get enough calcium if you don't eat dairy. It's in beans, tofu and a lot of vegetables too, especially leafy greens.

OILS

I'm sure you've already heard enough about fat in your life to be somewhat scared of it . . . We hear a lot about food products that are low fat or no fat—and sometimes it seems like there are one million weight loss programs that help you "lose the fat" and another million exercise programs that help you "burn the fat." It turns out that we actually need a certain amount of the right kinds of fat in order for the body and brain to have energy to function well. Fat helps cells do the important work of dividing and growing. Fat protects the organs of our bodies and helps keep us warm when it's cold, and fat helps our bodies absorb nutrients from what we eat. Fats are needed to produce the right amounts of hormones as well. There are a lot of healthy sources of fat such as olive oil or the oils that are found in walnuts and almonds and cashews. Avocado is a wonderful food to get healthy fat from, and it can be dressed up as guacamole, which is one of my absolute favorite ways to consume avocados! Foods that contain a lot of oil or anything that's fried in oil, such as chicken fingers and onion rings, have a high concentration of unhealthy oils, and you want to try not to eat those every day.

◆　◆　◆

Easy Yummy Guacamole

Here's an easy, fast way to make guacamole. Take an avocado (or two) and carefully cut it open. Scoop out the flesh and toss the gigantic pit! Mash it up really well with the back of a fork. Don't give up before it's all mashed! Add a pinch or two of salt, a tiny squirt or squeeze of lemon juice. Mash up a small garlic clove and add that, too. Mix it all together. Then, add a handful of any or all of these things to it before dipping a vegetable or cracker into it: chopped onion, tomato or cilantro. Yum!

Food Choices

There is so much talk about what kind of foods we should and shouldn't be eating. People tell us all sorts of things:

Eat more fruits and veggies.

Don't drink soda.

Eat whole grains.

Don't eat too much gluten.

Eat less red meat, but make sure you get enough protein.

Don't eat too many sweets, but don't deprive yourself.

Don't eat fast food . . . But what if that's what's easiest to get? And fast food tastes really good, and it's inexpensive, so what could be better, right? The thing to know about fast food is that it's full of a ton of sugar and salt; it also tends to have a lot of fat. It's the sugar, salt and fat that say to your brain, YUMMY! EAT ME! EAT ME!

The problem is that fast food and other foods that are high in carbs and salt and sugar make our bodies take in a lot more calories than we necessarily should in one meal. Over time, this can cause a lot of health problems and contribute to unwanted weight gain. I know you're thinking about the kids you know who eat a lot of fast food and are still skinny, right? Well, remember that for some bodies, weight gain won't happen right away, but it absolutely will catch up to you in your teen years or shortly after. And having a lot of fast food in your body can lead to very unhealthy insides, even if you look skinny on the outside. And we want healthy insides AND outsides!

In order to make healthier choices, some people adopt a particular way of eating that can help them make better food decisions. For example, in certain parts of the world, people believe that eating animals is unhealthy for their bodies and their spiritual selves, so they don't eat meat at all. In Japan and China, people historically live long and healthy lives, and they eat a lot of fish but no dairy and not a lot of red meat. In most every country in the world, the main source of protein is not meat, and the U.S. has the highest rates of weight problems, cancer, diabetes and heart problems. Countries that start eating like we do here in America, by importing our processed foods and opening fast food chains, eventually start having the same kinds of health problems we have here, so there is a definite connection there.

Because of this, some people have started adopting some variation of a vegetarian diet. Vegetarians tend to eat dairy and eggs, but no meat. Sometimes people will cut out meat but still eat fish, and those people are called pescatarians. People who follow a vegan diet (I'm one of them) don't eat any animal products at all. That means no meat, no fish, no dairy and no eggs. Being vegan or vegetarian is not impossible to do, but it does take a little bit of research so that you maintain your overall health. You can't just eat French fries all day and call yourself a vegan or vegetarian—you have to make sure you eat enough of a variety of healthy food to keep your body operating at its best.

Being vegetarian or vegan isn't for everyone, and that's fine. Remember this no matter how you eat: every meal is an opportunity to make good choices, and no one eats "perfectly" all of the time, so don't make it about perfection. See if you can expand your tastes and your mind enough to explore the possibility of making a commitment to your body to do the best you can for it, one meal at a time. Some people and even some schools in this country have been participating in "Meatless Mondays," which is a fun way to try out eating less meat as a start.

Usually, it's our moms and dads who decide what we eat most of the time. If your parents are anything like my parents, they do not want to hear you criticizing what they're feeding you. It's okay to tell your folks that you've been learning a bit about food and nutrition and maybe there are ways you can all make some healthy changes, as long as it fits into the budget. Chances are if you bring it up as a way to make everyone's eating better, it won't be seen as a criticism. And you can make the load lighter by offering to help with the shopping or the cooking or—better yet—the cleanup!

◆ ◆ ◆

Mindfulness

One of the most important things to consider whenever we eat anything is an amazing idea called mindfulness. This is exactly what it sounds like: being mindful and taking notice of what we're doing, no matter what it is. This idea has its roots in Eastern philosophy from thousands of years ago, and it's the basis of a lot of meditation and yoga practices, but it can apply to eating, too.

In many cultures and religious traditions, people pray before or after they eat, and although this may not work for some families, the idea is a smart one because it evokes a sense of mindfulness. Eating is something that many people in this world take for granted. Sadly, not everyone has access to the amount and kinds of foods we have access to. The next time you eat, take even just a second to acknowledge that you are grateful that you have food. If you want, be specific and acknowledge that whatever you are about to eat is something you hope will nourish your body and your life. It might feel silly at first to practice mindfulness in eating, but it's actually really cool to try to master.

Why is mindfulness important when we eat? Well, mindfulness encourages us to slow down. How many times do we just start shoveling food into our mouths at mealtime? I know I'm guilty of this! When we eat quickly, we tend to eat more than we should, and we often end up with an upset stomach from not giving our bodies time to catch up with digestion. Being mindful also helps us remember that eating is something we are part of, not just something that happens to us. Introducing moments of calm into whatever your mealtime looks like can help you see food as part of what keeps you going, and not something to take for granted.

Sending Messages to Your Brain

Did you know that it takes about 20 minutes for your brain to get the message that you've eaten enough to be full? When you eat, food hits your stomach, and your stomach sends signals to part of the brain called the hypothalamus, which is in charge of a bunch of things, like knowing when you're full. If you keep eating during the time it takes for the message to get to your hypothalamus, you end up continuing to eat before your brain can signal for you to stop. The way to stop this train is to slow down!

Exercise

Get some exercise! I know you probably hear this every day at school and maybe even at home, right?

Take a walk!

Find a sport!

Go run around!

Stop looking at your computer/the TV—get out of the house and move your body!

Okay, maybe that's just what my parents would shout at me, but I'm sure you know what I'm talking about. There are government programs designed to make us move our bodies and advertisements popping up everywhere reminding us to move more.

I'm not going to lie: they're all correct. Exercise and moving our bodies is something we need to do every day. For most of human history, people didn't have cars or taxis or buses or trains. Think about it: if they wanted to get somewhere, they walked. And even when people started building villages and then towns and cities, not everyone drove. People still walked a lot. Nowadays, many of us live in places where you can't really walk much of anywhere. Sure, you can walk around the block or in your neighborhood, but where I live, if I want to go to the market or get to a school or go meet my friends, I have to get in the car.

There are places around the world where walking to get around is the norm. And do you know what those places have in common? The people who live there are generally healthier. Turns out, walking releases endorphins from your brain which decreases your overall stress level and makes you feel calmer. People who live in places where they walk a lot tend to be in good shape; and I don't mean they're skinny because they burn so many calories walking all the time; they are healthier on the inside: They get sick less, they report feeling better in general, and they enjoy a life free of medical problems.

We have to create opportunities to move our bodies. Here are some ways to do that:

Walking is free, and it takes no equipment in order to make it happen. All you need is you and some shoes that feel good on your feet. Put on some headphones and walk even for 15 minutes. Walk around the block if you want to—if it's safe to do in your neighborhood. Any walking is good walking. I sometimes go walking on city streets, but keep in mind, city-street walking means you get stopped by traffic lights, and sometimes people have dogs that want to sniff you, and sometimes people walk too slowly in front of you and it can mess up your groove. But sometimes it's fun to see new things as I walk, as long as big, slobbery dogs don't bug me too much!

I also like to find places that are made for walking without cars and dogs and lots of people around. There are probably places in your city or town you've never explored, so get online and find out! Searching local parks or local trails is a great start. It's going to take a little bit of effort, but it's an investment in your body and your health. Do it!

Here's a walking tip: unless you like being alone or zoning out to music or a podcast, walking with a buddy is almost always better. My walking buddy and I can cover two or three times more ground if we walk together than if we walked alone because we laugh and talk along the way and we motivate each other. We set goals and give ourselves a little reward so we have something to work for. So we'll say, "After we walk 5 times, let's go to the movies." It makes it fun and gives us something to work toward.

If walking isn't for you, maybe you have a sport you're into, and that's terrific. If you're interested in getting into a sport, that's also terrific. Sports are a great way to move your body, because you work all sorts of muscles when you engage in them. If you do a team sport, you also get to socialize, which makes it more fun and takes your mind off of how hard you work to get your body moving.

Sports for Health

Being involved in a sport is a great way to support a healthy body and a healthy relationship with your body. Why?

- An obvious side effect of being involved in any sport is that you'll end up getting in shape, whether that's your reason for doing it or not. Whether it's running track, swimming laps or playing a team sport such as volleyball, softball or basketball, your body gets a great workout from being an athlete. Your body functions as a much more efficient fat-burning machine when you have a lot of muscle and less fat, which means you can actually worry less about calorie intake.

- Participating in a sport puts you in touch with your body in really healthy ways. You learn to make healthy choices about what foods best feed your body in order to be strong and fast, and you learn to have an appreciation for the amazing things your body can do.

Body Issues

Sometimes the things we experience as we transition from a girl to a young woman can be intimidating or scary. The changes of puberty combined with the new ways our bodies process food as we grow can be overwhelming, and the demands on our bodies to balance out the new curves and fat deposits we get—which are normal—can make us feel like we don't understand our bodies anymore. We spend so many years just having the body we have and often not thinking about it, and then—*BOOM!*—it changes, and it has different requirements, and clothes don't fit the same, and it can be really freaky. Boys—and even other girls—may make comments if your body changes quickly, or not quickly enough (as in my case!), and all of that attention can feel bad.

There are so many shapes and sizes of bodies, but when I look around, I mainly see one kind of body in the media: skinny. And not just skinny—*super* skinny. Seeing those images on TV and in movies and ads in magazines and on billboards can kind of mess up our minds. There are some bodies that are naturally free of fat and curves, and that's just how some girls and women are built. But for many of us, our bodies are not made to look like that—and if they did, we would be unhealthy. Did you know that the average dress size of women in the United States is actually a 16? The average dress size for models is a 0. That's less than a size 2! And did you know that almost every photo you see of a model has been "photoshopped"? That means computer editing takes out all of the things perceived as imperfections that many of us consider a normal part of our body, such as the curve of our belly or skin that pokes out of a bra strap. So the photos you see of models are not actually what those models even look like—imagine that! Here's a fun sketch of what models would look like if they actually had the body of your average American woman.

So what does it do to us when we see images that are so different from reality? Well, speaking from personal experience, it can make me feel like there's something wrong with me because I don't look like that. If every image I see looks like something I'm not, my brain takes that information in and says, "Hmmm . . . if everyone looks like that and I don't, there's something wrong with me." Pretty much everyone wants to fit in. And there may be a few exceptions, but for the most part, we want to be like other people at least a little bit. We don't want to feel left out, and when we do feel left out, we feel bad.

So what happens when we feel bad like this? Well, we want to make that bad feeling go away. The smartest thing we can do to make those bad feelings go away is to do things that make us feel good just the way we are. Surrounding ourselves with positive images of women in the media and embracing people we can look up to who support us loving ourselves is super important. So is finding supportive friends to talk to about our feelings.

However, what a lot of us do—myself included—is to try to find ways to make ourselves look like those people we see images of. Some girls start dieting at a very young age, and many feel shame about their bodies at a time when the body should be celebrated and enjoyed for being able to make you run and play and learn and grow.

It's healthy to want to make improvements to your appearance and your body, and if you are struggling with health problems or have spoken to a doctor about needing to make changes in your body, becoming aware of what size food portions are appropriate is a great start. Learning about how exercise can help burn calories and learning to practice mindfulness are also great things to do. It's important to know, however, that dieting can be very unhealthy, and it can also create a mental state of not being happy with where we're at, which can grow into a bigger problem.

Thinking you have to lose weight and always feeling you are fat even when you are at a healthy weight can develop into an eating disorder. Examples of eating disorders are anorexia, bulimia and binge eating.

Anorexia is thinking you have to lose weight and always feeling you are fat even when you are at a healthy weight. Anorexia is not just a way to diet; it starts with changes in your brain that get more problematic the more you restrict your eating, as the parts of your brain responsible for making decisions without thinking them through get confused. Anorexia can cause people to starve themselves so they don't get enough calories to keep their bodies working. When people are anorexic, they often skip meals, barely eat anything when they do eat or eat only very low-calorie foods.

Anorexics sometimes take laxatives or diet pills so that they lose more and more weight. These pills are very bad for your body and can lead to intestinal problems, severe dehydration, electrolyte imbalances that can cause organ failure, and even damage to your heart.

Remember how we have talked about the body needing a smart balance of carbohydrates, proteins and fats in order to stay healthy? Well, people who are anorexic aren't getting that balance. And because they're not, they might start getting sick a lot, their hair might start falling out, they may feel cold all the time, and their heart might even stop beating correctly because there isn't enough fuel in their body to keep it going. There are ways to have a healthy body without starving yourself. If you or someone you know is avoiding eating or restricting food as a way to get skinny, please get help.

Bulimia is an eating disorder that involves the very dangerous and harmful practice of making yourself throw your food up.

Sometimes in addition to throwing up food, girls will deprive themselves of food for days or weeks on end (like in anorexia) but then binge, eating large amounts of food at one sitting, even when not hungry, and hiding what they're eating. This is followed by feeling really guilty about it after. Bulimics who go on food binges will usually make themselves throw it all up again, and the cycle repeats over and over. (Sometimes girls will not throw up their food but will binge and then feel very guilty after; this is called binge eating disorder.) In addition to the danger of not having enough fuel in your body to make it function, bulimia can also cause stomach acid to burn sores into your throat and mouth and eat away at your teeth. Binging and purging is evidence of an unhealthy relationship between us and our food and our bodies and is not the key to beauty or happiness. If you or someone you know is doing any of these things, please get help.

There's also something called exercise bulimia. That's what it's called when people eat enormous amounts of food at one time and then exercise to a dangerous level, such as several hours a day, to lose the calories from the food that they ate. This can cause health problems such as having weak bones and being prone to injuries. Exercise is wonderful for the body, both inside and out, but counting calories in order to burn them off and exercising excessively is dangerous. Feeling guilty for not "burning off" all the calories you ate is not healthy. If you or someone you know is doing this, get help.

If you're looking for resources to help handle anorexia or

bulimia, either for yourself or for someone you know, here are a few places to look:

- Go to the NEDA website, NationalEatingDisorders.org and click on Find Help & Support.
- Visit the website for the National Association of Anorexia Nervosa and Associated Disorders at anad.org and click on the Get Help menu.
- Check out Eating Disorder Hope's website, EatingDisorderHope.com, and click into the Eating Disorder Treatment Centers section for resources listed by state.
- Take a look at the Resources section on the Elisa Project's website, TheElisaProject.org.

Body Image

Did you know that body image varies by culture? About 30,000 years ago, this lady was considered hot stuff:

Photo courtesy of Naturhistorisches Museum, Wien

© Museo Nacional del Prado.

In medieval Europe, women like these from Peter Paul Rubens's paintings were considered beautiful. In many cultures, women with strong bodies are considered beautiful even if they aren't skinny. The tennis-playing Williams sisters, Venus and Serena, have helped redefine what we see as beautiful. They are not skinny or a size 0 at all, but they are strong and fantastic.

Several advertising campaigns have started to use full-figured women to show that all body sizes should be represented and all body sizes can be beautiful. There are even full-figured runway models now who are inspiring women and girls of all ages to see themselves as worthy and deserving of positive attention, no matter what size they are.

There are now stores specializing in fashion for women who don't fit the "skinny" mold and advertisements by certain companies featuring women of all sizes. These are the kinds of changes we need to see so that we can appreciate all bodies, not just the ones we see on size 0 models.

Wrapping Up

With so much attention in the media being paid to dieting and how to look "perfect," it can sometimes seem like food is an enemy. Food should be enjoyable and should provide sustenance; exercise should lift our spirits and provide shapeliness to our souls and not just our muscles. I hope the adventure toward a healthy inside and outside is one I have inspired you to be excited about.

It is so important to feed your body so that it can grow as best as it can. The choices we make about how we eat, including being mindful and balancing life with a good amount of exercise, can increase not only our health but, more importantly, our understanding of our relationship to our body. Changes to your diet and lifestyle don't have to happen overnight; the first step toward a healthy body and mind starts with awareness about what you do, an understanding that making changes takes time and a willingness to be open to making healthier choices while forgiving yourself if you don't do it perfectly all the time.

Three

One of the neat things about growing up—and Girling Up—is that we get to learn all of the time. You're probably thinking, *Huh? It doesn't feel like I'm learning all of the time, and if I did have to learn all of the time, I definitely wouldn't think it was neat!* Well, guess what? The brain is made for learning even when we don't think we're learning. Mother Nature is sneaky that way; she is making sure we are fit for being strong, smart and spectacular whether we are consciously working on it or not!

Whenever we experience anything, it gets stored in our brain even if we don't consciously register it. There is a sea-horse-shaped region of the brain responsible for memory and learning called the hippocampus (*hippos* is Greek for "horse," and *kampus* is Greek for "sea monster"!). The hippocampus is made up of several layers of specialized cells, which are all bundled up like a strudel, making communication between all of the layers very fast and very efficient. When we experience something, the cells fire in specific ways to make an imprint in this region of the brain. When we need that information later on, the cells can refire and help us recall it.

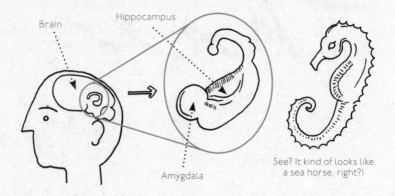

Brain

Hippocampus

Amygdala

See? It kind of looks like a sea horse, right?!

Now, not all experiences and memories are treated equally by the brain. Memories that have emotional content—such as the fact that I can remember everything my first-ever boyfriend, Josh Netburn, said to me and even what I was wearing the day we stood in the Hebrew-school hallway outside of our 4th-grade class and he broke up with me—are stronger and easier to recall details of. Memories associated with music or with a particular smell are also typically easier to recall, since they are made with extra information surrounding them, which adds to the strength of the memory as it is being stored, as well as increases the chance that it will be easier to recall later on. This is especially true for memories about very significant or emotional events.

This chapter is all about the ways we learn and what learning does to our brains and our bodies. We will talk about the learning we do in school and why it's important to go to school besides your parents saying you have to go. We'll talk about the physical and mental learning that goes on when we engage in sports, we'll discuss the kind of learning that happens when we watch TV or see a movie, and we will also explore what we can learn about ourselves through hobbies.

Learning Book Stuff: School

Some of us love school, while others would rather be anywhere but in a classroom! Some of us don't mind being in school because we get to hang out with our friends there, but the classes and homework part of it feels not as much fun as the hanging out with friends part. I get that. The opportunity that we have to learn in a school is actually a really special thing that not everyone in the world gets to experience, especially if you're female.

The Privilege of School

Imagine if you couldn't read or write. For millions of girls in the world, that's a reality. There are countries where schooling is not allowed for girls because they come from cultures that do not believe women need to be educated. Some cultures think that if women become too smart, they will not want to be married or do the things their family needs them to do. There is a brave and determined young woman named Malala Yousafzai who was injured when a group of terrorists specifically attacked a bus she was on because they didn't agree with her work. She was 15 at the time. Since recovering from her injuries, Malala has made it her life's work to ensure the right of girls everywhere to attend school. Education gives girls the opportunity to work, provide for themselves and not be dependent on marriage as a way to be taken care of, and it expands brain power in ways that can transform the world! We unfortunately live in a world where not all females are able to contribute equally. Young women like Malala are changing that, and the world will one day be a place of equal educational opportunity if we keep striving for it. (For more information, you can check out the Education for All Global Monitoring Report at unesco.org.)

Why do we go to school? Most people think we go there because we have to, and I guess we sort of do. But we actually go to school to learn the things we need to know so that we can leave high school with a certain set of skills. I know it may not always seem like it, but school is preparing you for life. No matter what kind of job you decide to have in your life, you will need to have basic training in how to read, how to understand and interpret what you read, and how to communicate, both in speech and in writing. A basic understanding of math is super important so that when you are a grown-up, you can manage your finances and go about life understanding how to handle and make decisions about money. That's the kind of stuff we learn in school.

Even though we are learning all of the time, it takes extra effort for some of us to see the beauty in learning. Take me as an example. I didn't start out with a love for learning math and science, and that lack of love continued all the way through middle school. I rushed through all of my math and science homework because I couldn't wait to get it over with, and I remember many evenings spent crying over fractions and word problems. I thought I was dumb because I could not seem to learn it, no matter how hard I tried. I thought that if I wasn't a "natural" at something in school, it meant nature was telling me, "This isn't for you!"

Once I got to high school, a miraculous thing happened that changed my life forever: I fell in love with biology. At the time, I was working on the TV show *Blossom*, and part of being a child actor meant I was tutored in all of my subjects on set. My biology tutor was studying to become a dentist; she tutored on the side to make extra money. I had never met someone so inspired by the world of science and math as Firoozeh. I wanted to be as passionate as she was about science. It took some catch-up to become a scientist, but my hard work paid off, and I am so grateful for the inspiration Firoozeh gave me.

Learning stuff in school may not always come easy, but the possibility exists for you to challenge yourself and work toward anything you want to be. Finding the way you learn best is a key to opening that door to the future. If you are struggling with learning, consider talking to a teacher you like, even if they don't teach the subject you're struggling in. See if they can help you figure out what ways you might best learn the things you are having a hard time with. It's worth the effort—I am living proof of that.

Here are some of the tips I have gathered over my years in school for learning success.

1. **Don't skip class.** It may seem like it totally doesn't need to be said, but I'm going to say it anyway: do NOT skip classes. I know you may not be able to say you'll NEVER skip class, but here's the thing: the best way to learn is to be where the learning is happening. Once we start a habit of cutting class or not valuing putting our butts in seats in a classroom, we start a pattern of falling behind and needing to play catch-up, which makes

learning hard. Consistency is key for the brain to make the most of a learning environment. Treat school as if you're getting paid to be there, as if it's your job. And if you think about it, someday, the job you have that pays your bills and buys you a house and the car you already know you want will come from the time you put in right now going to class and being in school. So get to class like your life depends on it—it kind of does!

2. **Keep an assignment notebook.** Staying organized and on top of assignments makes it easier to learn best. Get a small notebook and decorate it with stickers or drawings—anything to personalize it and make it truly yours. Every day you're in school and an assignment is handed out, make a list and write down when it's due. Even if the teacher hands it out on a printout or directs you to an online syllabus, put it down in your own handwriting anyway. Writing things down makes your brain think about them and remember them in a new way. Nerdy fact about me: all through middle school and high school, I would color coordinate my assignment notebook with a different color pen for each subject. That may not be your thing, but whatever you can do to make your assignment notebook and schedule of "what's

due when" clear and organized will help you a ton in getting it all done!

3. **Don't procrastinate.** Although there may sometimes be reasons you can't do your homework right away and some brains need a break before tackling homework after a long day at school, you learn best if you can practice the things your teachers talk about pretty soon after they talk about them. Doing homework close to when the subject matter was introduced in class means your brain will take the information most available and commit it to memory most reliably.

4. **Learn to say no to distraction.** There will be a lot of distractions that will try to get between you and school and homework, and every distraction takes away from the brain's power to master something. Our brains need a clear and simple message when they're trying to learn. Text messages asking you to hang out rather than do homework, or even just the pinging notifications on your phone saying that you have messages waiting to be read, get in the way of your hippocampus doing its job. Say no to distraction by turning off your phone and the TV during study time, and you'll get more done and get it done best for success later.

5. **Repeat it again and again.** And again. One of the most important factors in learning and memory is repetition. The more times we think about something or study something, the more reliably it will be stored in long-term memory. Flash cards can be used to learn just about any subject, and they can be reviewed anytime, anywhere. Making lists of things to memorize is also a great way to engage the motor system (writing) in the memory process. This makes for stronger memory formation and better learning and recall when it's time for a test.

6. **Get creative.** Don't just read to learn, engage other parts of your brain and body in the process! Writing and rewriting important words and facts engages your brain in ways that increase stimulation for the hippocampus and encourages it to remember all of those important details your teacher will quiz you on. Another hippocampus-stimulating trick to optimize learning is to make facts you need to memorize into songs. Introducing a musical component to learning hits the hippocampus extra hard and makes for strong memories of things like the order of the planets, which I only remember because my 8th grade science teacher sang the order to a really catchy song with an easy-to-remember melody. Be creative, and your hippocampus will reward you!

Learning About Playing: Sports

We don't just learn "school stuff" as we Girl Up. We learn skills that add to our personalities and our lives in general. When we participate in a sport, we are training our body to learn a set of skills, but we are also combining those physical skills with a corresponding mental set of skills. This makes for powerful learning in mind and body. In sports, we learn not only how to throw or catch or run or jump, but we also learn about setting goals and meeting expectations. We learn to manage time to meet deadlines, and we find ways to use practice time to enhance our athletic outcomes. We have to learn to cope with losing and also with winning; we learn to be sensitive and compassionate because of the interactions athletes are constantly having with others. We also learn how to work well with others, taking into account their strengths, weaknesses and needs, which is one of the most important skills you can learn—you'll need it for the rest of your life! So if you want to strengthen your brain, challenge it with sports and learn a ton that will benefit you inside and out.

Learning About Culture: Media

One of my favorite things to do when I was a tween and a teenager was to go to the movies. The experience was really exciting, from the popcorn and snacks to the sort of magical feeling you get when you sit in a dark theater and a gigantic movie plays in front of you.

I was mesmerized by it. Getting lost in the fantasy world of movies is something I loved as a kid and teenager, and it's something I still love as an adult. The same is true of television. When I was your age, I typically watched a few hours of television every weeknight—but only after my homework was done. On the weekends, my brother and I would watch cartoons in the mornings while my parents got to sleep in. Very rarely, we would find a family movie to watch, either because we happened upon it on a night we all were able to be there, or by renting a movie from the video store (it was like having Netflix in our neighborhood!).

I had no idea that all of those movies and TV shows were adding to my learning; I thought I was just having fun and being distracted from school and chores. It turns out that the way the brain works, we don't just use our hippocampus for learning facts and figures; we also use it to store emotional memories and experiences—including things we see and experience when we watch movies and TV—that become a part of our brains and, in some way, make up who we are for the rest of our lives.

When I think about my childhood and teen years, I specifically remember NOT being allowed to watch a lot of things that I wanted to watch. You see, my parents were pretty strict about what movies and TV shows I could watch, and there were many times when I missed out on movies and shows that my friends were watching because my parents were concerned about language, violence and nudity. It bummed me out big time. I still remember kids giving me a hard time for not being able to go to certain movies with them. It was embarrassing!

Now that I am a mom and have kids of my own, I understand what a delicate juggling act it is to be a parent and how much of our time watching movies and television is teaching us things about our culture and the world. Parents want to have control over what their kids see and learn, and that definitely makes sense. But as someone who was not allowed to see certain TV shows and movies, I'm going to tell it to you straight: it's really a bummer when everyone is allowed to see movies that you're not allowed to see. I have no magic that can make your parents change their minds, though. What I can say is that even if it seems like a big deal when it happens, in a few years it won't matter at all. I hope you believe me!

I frequently tell my sons that there are certain things that exist in the world that are really intense and that, once you see them, you can't unsee them. Now that you know a bit about the hippocampus, I'm sure you agree that that's true. There is a time and a place to learn everything, and your brain knows this. Everyone has different levels of sensitivity to different things. Have you ever seen a movie or a TV show that made you cry because it was so sad and emotional, but you watched it with a friend who had absolutely no reaction to it? Have you ever seen something in a movie or on TV that was really upsetting and made your stomach hurt, but other people who saw it didn't find it upsetting at all? How about this: have you ever seen something on the news that made you feel yucky and grossed out, but the person you saw it with felt totally fine? That's because everyone is different.

Why are we different this way? Well, part of it is just genetics.

We inherit not only eye color and hair color and a genetic plan for how tall we will be, but also the ability to process emotional information in a certain way. Some people are super resilient, and they don't feel affected by emotional stuff much at all, while other people are more sensitive, and they feel very affected by emotional stuff. Neither of these are the right or wrong way to be. They are just different.

The things we learn when we watch movies and television are significant, and they do matter. It is the job of parents to protect

How Much Screen Time Is Too Much?

After many years of research and analysis, the American Academy of Pediatrics has officially announced that screen time should be limited to under two hours per day. Yup: *two hours a day*. We end up pushing aside physical activity, social interactions and schoolwork when we engage more with our screens than with the outside world. As an experiment, keep track of how many hours you spend a day on your computer or in front of the TV. Find ways to be selective about the time you spend with your screen and see if you can feel a difference in your life. You might be surprised!

children as much as is reasonable and possible from things that might upset them or hurt them or introduce them to concepts that they are just not ready for. This might be why your parents don't let you watch a certain kind of movie or TV show. They may have knowledge of ways you have reacted to similar things in the past, and they may not feel that you're ready to handle something until you have a bit more knowledge and maturity.

Learning About Yourself: Hobbies

Even though I was very social when I was Girling Up, there were a lot of times in my life that I wasn't around tons of friends. I remember times when I would tell my mom and dad I was bored, and they never liked hearing that at all! I spent a good amount of time when I was little playing outside and riding my bike, but once I hit the tween years, riding my bike just didn't have the same appeal it did when I was younger.

One of the things I started to cultivate as I entered middle school was hobbies. Now, when you think of hobbies, I bet you think of some old lady sitting on a rocking chair knitting. Or maybe you think of a loner teenage girl doing puzzles by herself. The fact is, hobbies are interests we have that we can pursue alone, but sometimes we pursue them with others. Hobbies can involve learning a skill or a set of skills, doing crafts or playing a musical instrument. Hobbies can be playing board games, collecting comic books or learning all about a particular historical period.

So, what are some of my hobbies? Well, I started playing the piano in kindergarten and have continued playing to this day. I write some of my own songs, but mostly I like to learn music that I enjoy listening to, playing and singing along to anything from The Beatles to Adele and everything in between. I learned how to play trumpet in my elementary school when I was 10, and I continued to play in orchestra and jazz band through middle school. I learned bass guitar when I was 16 and played with a few bands in my college years, although I was a very shy performer, so that didn't last long! Music is a wonderful hobby and it is also a terrific outlet for emotional release. In addition, the brain does amazing things when mastering music. Musical ability has been linked to advanced math ability as well as increased creativity in other fields. It's never too late to learn an instrument, and I know this because I learned how to play the harp on *The Big Bang Theory* just a few years ago!

Another hobby I have is sewing. I was raised by a mom who knew how to sew really well—her parents were both tailors—and my mom passed on her love of sewing to me by teaching me the different kinds of stitches, how to assemble clothing patterns and how to make blankets and pillows for my dolls. The things my mother taught me were invaluable: she taught me using math, geometry and color theory, but she made it fun, interesting and inspiring. Some of the most memorable times I had with my mom as a child were learning with her—not just learning how to sew, but learning alongside her. That's kind of how learning works: learning things with others is its own process of learning. We learn skills, but we also learn about interaction, relationships and what we like and don't like.

As I got older, even though I didn't play with dolls anymore, my love of sewing and being crafty stayed with me. The things I learned were a source of inspiration for me even as a tween and teenager, when I made necklaces and bracelets for myself and my friends. I took inspiration from what was trendy, found bead stores in my neighborhood and asked the people working there for help in imitating the trends. I went from threading beads onto string to using more sophisticated wire thread, adding clasps to make my jewelry look more polished and using more sophisticated designs.

I've dabbled in a lot of other crafty hobbies, such as painting with acrylics, making pot holders, learning calligraphy, trying out papier-mâché and weaving friendship bracelets. My sons and I have started trying out something called felting, where you use a felting needle to turn a ball of wool into amazing and elaborate shapes, like animals and even people. I recently started working with epoxy resin to make paperweights with beads, flowers and glitter floating in them!

Hobbies use learned skills as a springboard for imagination and creativity. Your brain thrives on new stimulation as well as your ability to incorporate learned information that may seem simple, but with a little creative input, can delight and bring joy. That's the most rewarding kind of learning you can experience.

My Things

Here are some of my hobby creations, starting from when I was your age.

Here's a necklace I made after seeing a similar style of necklace for sale in a really expensive boutique. I think they were $100 and I knew I could never afford that, so I made my own for far less than it would have cost to buy one!

Here is a blanket my mom helped me make for my dolls. My sons used them for their dolls when they were little.

These are examples of the pot holders my family made, which my mom and I still like to make. She used to sew together about 12 of these to make rugs out of them.

This is one of the paperweights I made. I made this by pouring some stinky, sticky resin, so it requires an adult's help, but it's really fun!

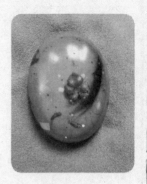

Here's the first thing my sons and I felted: a little snowman wearing earmuffs. Isn't he cute?

Wrapping Up

Our brains are made for learning: how to survive, how to communicate, how to exist as humans on a very complicated planet. The way we learn in school can transform our lives, and the exercise we give our brains as we learn makes them stronger, smarter and more able to adapt to new situations with grace and ease.

Learning how to play sports, how to understand information received through the media and how to do things that bring us and others joy are beautiful examples of the unbelievable uniqueness of being human. We are learning beings, and we are creative beings. Good school habits, making wise choices about your free time and learning new ways to occupy your hands and mind will lead to you being a well-rounded person equipped to deal with whatever life delivers next.

Four

• HOW WE LOVE •

One of the most amazing things about being human is that we can have close relationships with other people. Think about it for a second: there are hundreds of thousands of animals on the planet, and mammals like us get to have really complicated and very meaningful relationships with others.

As mammals, we form the closest bonds with other mammals, and in the case of *Homo sapiens* (which is what we are!), relationships are defined by intimacy. We are capable of having intimate significant relationships with our parents, our siblings and other family members, as well as friends and romantic partners.

So what exactly is intimacy? When you hear the word *intimacy*, you might think of the kind of relationship you'd have with a boyfriend or a girlfriend or a husband or wife, but intimacy is actually a general term that refers to a kind of extreme closeness where we share aspects of ourselves that we wouldn't share with just anybody. Intimacy means being in a relationship where we're making ourselves vulnerable and so is the other person. Intimate relationships allow us to learn new things about ourselves, to challenge ourselves to be patient, affectionate and compassionate, and to appreciate other people's viewpoints. Intimacy means we have the capacity to engage with others in meaningful ways.

Let's Get Close: Family and Friends

The first intimate relationships we have in our lives are with our caregivers, who, for most people, are parents. Some babies are raised with help from grandparents or older siblings or other family, and some babies are raised with the help of a nanny. No matter who changes our diapers or feeds us or gives us baths, the first people we come in contact with when we're tiny are our first and, in some ways, most important intimate relationships.

Even though we probably can't remember the first months and even years we were alive, the way people talked to us, the way people held us and the way people attended to our needs made a big difference. Babies rely on caregivers to understand what their cries mean, and they need to trust that someone will help them when they need help. Sometimes a baby's cry means "I'm hungry!" and sometimes it means "My diaper is really wet and kind of mushy right now!" but other times it means "I'm feeling lonely—hold me!" So even as babies, we are genetically programmed to want to be understood, and we have an innate sense of trust that someone will both understand us and be able to help us get our needs met. That's actually the core of any good relationship, and it starts when we're too young to even remember it!

As we get older, we have meaningful relationships with the people who continue to feed us, provide us with clothing and a place to live, help us grow and learn new things and have fun with us. For many of us, our parents, siblings and extended family are our main relationships when we're little. When we start going to school, we make friends and form new relationships with people our own age, and we find that  we want to pursue relationships with people who have the same interests as we do. We want to participate in conversations about things we have in common, and we start to open up to people about our dreams, our hopes and even our fears. These are relationships that are close and meaningful. They are intimate.

One of the most-often-talked-about close relationships we have in our lives is with a best friend. A best friend is typically the person we are closest to, whom we share a lot in common with and can tell anything to. A best friend helps navigate the most thrilling and challenging parts of being alive. In the teen years, it sometimes becomes more and more clear who we can best rely on, and our idea of what makes the best "best friend" may even change over time. That's totally normal, and it's important to remember that people come into our lives to help us along in our journeys, but they may not always play the same role throughout our entire lives. A best friend should be someone we can trust with private information, someone who has our interests at heart and someone we share values with. Best friends support each other even if they don't agree with each other all of the time, and they care about each other very deeply. Finding a best friend is a wonderful thing, but if you don't have a bestie, that's okay too; there are lots of ways to be close to people and to get support, even if you spread it out over a few friends.

Friend or Foe?

Sometimes friendships can get confusing. Our trust may get violated, or we start to question whether someone is really looking out for our best interests. Here are some questions about friendships you may have. These are warning signs that a friendship might need some help. If you answer yes to most of these questions, you may need to redefine it to protect yourself from getting hurt.

- Does your friend tell other people things about you that you've asked her to keep private?

- Do you have a friend who sometimes seems more interested in the things you have rather than what you bring to the relationship, such as wanting to ride in your car, use your cool new headphones or hang out at your pool?

- Do you feel like she acts one way when it's just the two of you but totally different when other people are around?

- Does she try to pressure you into doing things you don't want to do, such as smoke, use drugs, drink or do other dangerous things?

- Does your friend threaten to end the relationship if you don't agree with her/do the things she is doing?

- Does your friend tease other people and assume you will go along with it even if it feels wrong to you?

- Does your friend consistently tell you about plans she has made with other friends that you were left out of in order to make you jealous?

- Do you feel weird or bad after hanging out but can't put your finger on why?

If any of these things sounds familiar, you may want to talk to a trusted adult about the kinds of friendships that are healthy and can help you be the best you that you can be.

Relationships change throughout your life. My brother and I did a lot of things together when we were little, but as he got older and his interests spread out from mine, we had fewer moments of intimate connection and more moments of just being siblings in the same family, which is normal and also fine. I was super close with my mom and dad when I was little, but as I made friends and found things I liked to do, I spent less time with them and more time in my room reading and playing with friends. This is also normal!

It is healthy for relationships to change, and the great thing about strong intimate relationships with family and friends is that there is always a solid core of connection to come back to. There have been times as an adult when I needed my brother almost more than I needed him when we were kids, even though we haven't been as close all of these years. We can draw on our connection as adults in new and important ways now.

The intimacy we feel with family and friends is special and valuable. It is the foundation of all of the relationships we end up having with new people we meet as we grow. Some of the people we meet will become part of a separate kind of intimate relationship: a romantic intimate relationship.

Let's Get Even Closer: Romance

Writing this section of the book made me blush a lot because even though I'm an adult, romance is still kind of a funny thing to talk about. I remember having crushes on so many people when I was a teenager, and as a grown adult, I still have crushes—it's a part of being human, no matter how old you are. With a crush, there's an excitement you feel in your stomach and a nervousness you have when you're around the person you are crushing on. Crushes are a way that our brains and bodies start getting us used to the idea of liking someone enough to think we might be interested in getting closer to them. Crushes can start because we think someone is cute or funny or just really super cool, and crushes are the earliest stages of romantic intimacy, which is what happens if a crush develops into dating and all of the stuff that comes along with dating.

A lot of what you experience when you are feeling romantic about someone has a basis in the brain and the body. The brain releases chemicals to our bodies when we have romantic feelings, and these feelings can be very powerful. And if you're experiencing them for the first time, they can also be kind of scary!

When you feel romantically interested in someone you might feel nervous around them. These are some of the things that might happen when you're nervous:

- Sweating, especially the palms of the hands and underarms
- Dry mouth
- A flushed face and lips that may feel kind of warm and may look pink or red (This is called blushing!)
- An increased heart rate, sometimes to the point that it feels like the heart is going to beat right out of your chest
- Having difficulty finding words . . . stuttering, stammering and sometimes sort of babbling

- Feeling disoriented, as if we don't know what is going on or who else is around besides the person we are focusing on

All of these things are normal responses to being attracted to someone. The nervous system is sending information to the body to indicate that there is excitement going on. When that happens, adrenaline (a hormone) is sent out from the brain to increase heart rate and blood flow—that's responsible for the blushing and rapidly beating heart and also the sweating. The "out of it" feeling is caused by a sort of overload that the brain experiences when there is a lot of exciting input happening at once. If we're focusing on someone's beautiful clear blue eyes or their adorable freckles, our brain sometimes has a hard time also managing to multiply fractions or remember who was the prime minister of France in 1879 (William

Waddington!). It can feel really disorienting to have our brain so taken over by feelings, but that's just the way it is—and it's how Mother Nature designed it.

Get Ready for Hormones

When we really like someone or find someone really attractive, our brains produce a group of special hormones that make our bodies feel good. It's those feel-good hormones that make us want to spend more time with that person so that we can experience more of that feeling good more of the time. This is the basis for wanting to be around someone when we like them!

Serotonin is the hormone that is responsible for making us feel super good, and the feeling of "walking on air" when we are with someone we like is due in part to this hormone. If you've ever felt over the moon about someone, you know what I'm talking about. Oxytocin is the hormone that's released in a way that makes your stomach feel like it's turning upside down when you see someone you like. Oxytocin is also responsible for acting on parts of the body that are involved in the biological process of romantic relationships. So feeling a sensation of "heat" in your chest and in your genital region is often a part of being attracted to someone. It doesn't *always* happen, but it's pretty normal if it does.

Dopamine is a powerful hormone that is released when people have a strong need to be with someone and they get the opportunity to do that. It's known as a "reward" hormone, because it's the body's way of rewarding us with good feelings for doing something we have been working hard to do. This hormone is special because it has an addictive quality; we want to feel a rush of dopamine over and over again once we've gotten a taste of it. This hormome is what makes us seek out our crush over and over again!

Magnetic Feelings: Attraction

How do we know who we will find attractive? How can we prepare for that? Or can we?!

Let's take a step back from the idea of romance and think about what makes someone attractive at all.

What do *you* find attractive?

When I was in middle school, most girls I knew liked guys who were athletic and tall and muscle-y (or as muscle-y as 14-year-old guys can be . . . !). Blond hair for guys was "in," and a lot of girls were interested in tan guys who took good care of their hair and clothes, and wore cologne. The first time I ever had serious romantic feelings for someone was in the 8th grade. He was a pretty scrawny, pale-skinned 13-year-old with half-shaved messy black hair, who possibly didn't even look in the mirror every day and didn't ever wear cologne. His name was Mischa, and he liked punk rock and wore a leather jacket. I composed poems for him, picked flowers for him and sat 15 feet away from him in the hallways at recess and lunch for years—even through high school—hoping he'd notice me. He never really did.

Even though Mischa looked and acted so differently from what most other girls I knew thought was attractive, it was very clear to me why I thought the sun rose and set on his green eyes and wacky shaggy hair: he was very smart, he was really funny, and he had a way of doing his own thing and not caring if other people didn't like it, which I thought was spectacular.

I tell this story about my affection for Mischa to illustrate an important point: attraction is highly variable. Sure, there are certain things that are universally considered attractive, but there are also a lot of variations on attractiveness depending on what country you live in, what year it is, what religious tradition and cultural background you're from and what images you see on TV and in the movies. Just like everyone has different favorite colors or favorite foods, we also have different things we find interesting or attractive in other people.

In addition, what's considered attractive in America is not what's necessarily considered attractive in Africa or China or South America or in Polynesia. Women with rounder bodies are celebrated many places in the world, while here in the United States, the images we see in the media make a lot of us feel like we can never be too skinny, even when it's not healthy for us.

Here's the thing: there are no rules about what attractive is, and sometimes we can't even figure out why we feel googly-eyed when we are around someone we like. Some people find brains far more important than beauty, and sometimes we will find something attractive that, a year from now, we can't even imagine finding attractive! The notion of what makes someone attractive is not simply how they make our genitals feel; it's about a lot more than that. Sometimes someone with a smart brain and a wicked sense of humor stirs something in our soul that makes us feel like we want to be around that person all of the time, no matter what they look like. And sometimes someone will be so physically attractive that they will make us feel drawn to them, but when we find out that they are mean or cruel or have no manners, they will all of a sudden seem really unattractive. Thank goodness there are no rules about any of this, because even though no one else understood my affection for Mischa, it was a special time in my life to feel those things and experience them. I'm glad I didn't let other people's opinions govern my behavior.

Dating

Now that we understand a little bit better what attraction is and what it does to our bodies and brains, let's talk about what happens after we are attracted to someone. In most cultures, the next step after attraction is dating, which means different things to different people and also varies a lot depending on where you live or where your family is from.

Dating generally means spending concentrated time with

someone we are attracted to, but for most of human history, romantic love or being attracted to someone was not a requirement for dating. I know that must sound strange, but parents used to set their kids up with a mate for life based on arrangements between the families. Sometimes marriages were basically business agreements between two fathers regarding their kids. Women were essentially treated as property, and they usually didn't get a vote as to who they would marry. There are many communities in the world where arranged marriage is still the way couples get together. In addition, for much of human history, men were allowed to have more than one wife, and there are still places where men can have more than one wife, such as parts of the Middle East, Asia, Africa and Australia.

Most of us meet a lot of prospective romantic partners at school, through community activities, through extracurriculars and through hanging out with friends. I spent a lot of time in my middle school and high school years in malls, arcades and friends' living rooms chatting with all of the boys I had crushes on. But dating has changed a lot since I was in school. Because of smartphones and social media, dating now involves texting and following, liking and commenting on the different

things people post online. You can learn a lot about someone from online profiles in ways I never could when I was dating. There are some great things about that, but there are some challenges, too.

Even though your parents must look like dinosaurs to you, they were your age around 30 years ago, and considering that *Homo sapiens* have been around for about 200,000 years, 30 years isn't that long ago! But the thing that makes talking about dating so hard is how much it changes all of the time—there have been so many changes just in the years since your parents and I were your age. Here's a rundown of what dating used to be like and what it's like now, with a special emphasis on making the most of the good changes while learning to navigate the potentially problematic changes.

NICE TO MEET YOU

THEN: It used to be that you dated people from your social circles: people you knew from school or your family's religious events or from sports teams or clubs you belonged to. Chances are, if you met someone, your parents already knew them, and if your parents didn't, someone in your family or circle of friends did.

NOW: There are so many ways to meet people! Besides meeting people at school and at extracurricular activities, you can meet online. Social-media platforms and comments sections are virtual hangout spaces, an entire world of online communities where people now connect, and are a place to meet.

PRECAUTIONARY POINTERS: Meeting people online can be a neat way to expand the circle of people you know and can date, but keep in mind that the way people present themselves online is not always the way they actually are, and in some cases, people blatantly lie about who they are, how old they are and what they're all about. Sometimes people make things up about themselves so they can get you interested in them. In addition, the way people share about themselves online can make us feel like we know them but, in reality, we don't. That's just the nature of the online beast!

HOW TO BE SMART ABOUT IT: If you meet someone online, the best way to really get to know if that someone is potentially a good date, or even just a possible new friend, is to meet them in person—but only with your parents' knowledge and consent. You should never go out with someone you met online without an adult knowing where you are. Anyone who asks you to keep a secret about meeting up with them should for sure be avoided. That's what we call in my house a "prickly" person; prickly people ask you to keep secrets from those close to you, and they are not safe people to hang out with.

COURTSHIP: WHAT'S THAT?!

THEN: *Courtship* is the old-fashioned word for the way two people who are dating get to know each other. The super old-school version of this sounds like a TV show from the 1950s: a young man comes to a girl's house with flowers and sits and chats with her dad while she finishes getting ready. The idea is that the guy is supposed to impress the girl and her family, and their dating is an elaborate way for him to show he has good intentions and wants to spend more time with her, eventually landing him the chance to ask her father if he has the permission to marry her.

While the idea that a guy needs a girl's dad's approval to date her and marry her sounds so out of date and kind of absurd, what is kind of sweet about the notion of courtship is this: it takes time to get to know someone. It takes time to see what it's like to be together if you're interested in a more serious relationship. It takes time to build up trust in order to let someone see more of you and to eventually engage in an intimate or romantic relationship that at some point may involve hand holding, kissing and—yes, eventually many people choose to be sexually intimate! And this kind of courtship shows that it is important for your family to know the person you're dating and for them to spend time together at some point.

NOW: This is an area of dating that is completely different in almost every way compared to how it used to be! While there are still places in the world where a guy comes to the door to pick a girl up for a date and chats with her dad before he can take her out, a lot of courtship does not look anything like that anymore. Courtship now sometimes means rarely actually talking; texting and sending each other pictures may be a large part of the courtship process. Many people think that dating should not be a stepping-stone to a serious relationship, but should just be for fun.

PRECAUTIONARY POINTERS: What's potentially problematic about the loss of a notion of courtship is that we basically think we can and should trust people before we even know much about them. People may say things we want to hear, but we have no idea if they plan to follow through with promises, since they haven't necessarily had to put time and effort in to show that they are reliable or faithful or honest. It can be confusing and hard to know who to trust sometimes.

Also, an aspect of the courtship process that never existed before now is sending someone you like pictures of yourself. While this may sound totally fine, as you get older, the idea of sending "sexy" pictures may seem like a good idea. After all, we see so many celebrities posting pictures of themselves on their social media accounts in lingerie, skimpy bathing suits and sometimes even naked! It's no wonder a lot of young women have started doing the same when they want to appeal to someone they are interested in.

The problem with sending sexy pictures or sexting with someone (talking about sexy stuff in texts) is that the pictures you send could live forever on someone's phone, because they might not delete them even if they said they would. Pictures you send to one particular person might end up being shared with a bunch of people you didn't want to have see your picture. This can be embarrassing, and in some cases, it can make people pick on you, tease you or start rumors about you that can be hard to shake; it may even become legally complicated if the person uses your photos in ways you didn't know they would. The notion of "modesty" may seem really out of date, but more and more young women are maintaining a sense of privacy and modesty in dating and even in clothing choices. (See the box for more on this!)

HOW TO BE SMART ABOUT IT: The more time you spend with someone in person—and not just texting—the better you can see if you like actually being with them. Having a friendship or relationship that involves sharing pictures and flirting is fun, but you want to make sure that there is a good amount of time spent in person seeing how you feel when the two of you are together. In addition, some of that old-fashioned courtship stuff is nice; it can show you that you are worthy of someone's time and respect. That's actually a really important aspect of dating for both people involved. The kinds of relationships you want to have will be with people you like spending time with and people you can trust with your feelings; it's best to see who wants to put that effort in early on!

Modesty

What does it mean to be modest? Most people think it's about how you dress, and "modest" clothes may make you think of high-collared shirts and long skirts that you usually see only religious women wearing. *Modesty* is actually a broader word, and it means reserving parts of yourself as private and special, both in how you dress and how you behave. Wendy Shalit wrote a really neat book about this called *A Return to Modesty*, and she describes how a lot of young women (the age of all of you reading this book!) are starting to think differently from the way a lot of us are told to behave in our society today. The idea that the way to show your feminine side is by wearing short skirts and lots of makeup may not work for everyone. She talks about campaigns led by young girls to try to get clothing stores to sell more options for girls who don't want to wear short shorts or tank tops all the time. She also does a really good job of discussing how the way we share ourselves on the internet can have a negative impact on our reputation and even future decisions. If you're a girl who craves more coverage from your clothes and doesn't want to share everything online, you may want to check out her book. It's really inspiring!

LET'S TALK ABOUT *S-E-X*

In Chapter One, we talked about the mechanics of the female body and how our ovaries produce an egg every month or so that, when presented with a sperm, may develop into a baby. How this actually happens is that the penis fills up with blood because of a state of excitement called "arousal." Arousal makes the penis become hard, and this is called an erection. When a female is aroused, her nipples sometimes stand up a little bit, and blood flows into her vagina, particularly into the clitoris, which we discussed in Chapter One. An erect penis fits inside of the vagina in such a way that it releases sperm in an act called ejaculation. The sperm is released into the highest part of the vagina near where it meets the uterus at a location called the cervix (reference diagram on page 17). Ejaculation produces millions of sperm (they are very tiny, so they take up about one teaspoon) whose goal it is to find an egg to fertilize. Once an egg is fertilized, it can implant in the uterus and begin forming what will in about 9 or 10 months become a human baby.

The process is amazing, and it is a very exciting and unbelievable thing to be able to grow a life inside of your body! However, having a baby is an enormous responsibility and it takes time, maturity and a lot of financial and emotional resources to be able to be a parent.

Let's talk about how people have behaved surrounding the issue of sex and how you can prepare for one day deciding how you want to handle sex and all that it entails.

THEN: Historically, people of certain religious and cultural backgrounds—as well as a lot of others not from a particular religious or cultural background—have waited to have sex until they are married, and for your grandparents' and great-grandparents' generations, that was not unusual at all. The idea that your body is a sacred place may sound weird now, but for a lot of history, being sexually intimate with someone was considered in many communities to be something you didn't do until marriage. Of course there have always been people who have been sexually active before marriage, but one of the main reasons the act of sex was saved for marriage is the simple fact that women are very likely to get pregnant if they have sex! It's just a biological fact. Until very recently, women's reproductive cycles determined a lot about their lives, so sex was seen as a way to make babies, which for most cultures is encouraged to be done in the context of marriage so that a woman can be provided for while she cares for her babies. Many religions and cultures made a big deal over seeing sex as "forbidden," often because of the possibility of getting pregnant outside of marriage. In certain religious traditions, such as Catholicism and some Eastern religions, leaders of the faith take vows of celibacy (not having sex) for part of their lives and sometimes for their entire lives, because sex is seen as a potential distraction.

NOW: There are still many people who believe that sex is something you save for marriage, but for many young women in this country, there has been a real shift in the past 60 years in how we see ourselves and how we behave sexually. There are many reasons for this shift, and one of them is that in 1960, a birth control pill (referred to as "the Pill") was introduced that could stop women from releasing an egg, thus making it possible for them to control when they got pregnant—or didn't. The Pill changed the world in ways we are still learning to understand. Since the 1960s and what is sometimes called the "sexual revolution," the notion of "waiting for marriage" has shifted a lot for many women.

What this looks like is that a lot of girls and young women— many of you reading this book, actually—may be comfortable with things that girls and young women even 15 years ago would not have been comfortable with. Kissing used to be something many of your parents wondered if they "should" do on a first date, and now I'm sure you know that kissing can happen before you even decide that you are dating! Hooking up is something that sometimes happens even between people with no interest in dating. Having sex is seen by some as not a big deal and some people think it's something you should do just because it feels good.

PRECAUTIONARY POINTERS: It would be super awkward for me to just come right out and say, "Don't hook up with people you barely know!" "Wait until you know someone before you let them kiss you!" "Don't have sex before you're in a committed relationship!" I know for a lot of people that's not going to make sense, and I get that. Here's the truth: every time you come in physical contact with someone by kissing them, touching them or being sexually intimate with them, you are opening yourself up to the history of who they have been intimate with. Even when we just kiss someone and share body fluids—which is what happens when we kiss!—our bodies have ways they react.

Anytime you are sexually intimate with someone, even by kissing, that's something to keep in mind. I'm not saying that if you kiss someone, you're going to get sick, but the principle is important to know: being intimate in a sexual way is sharing parts of you that can be affected physically in sometimes very serious ways, because coming in contact with someone's penis or vagina or having body fluids exchanged through kissing, oral sex and sexual intercourse is a very significant experience for the body. A great example is that if someone kisses a person who has a cold sore and then they kiss you, you may end up with the cold sore. Anytime anyone's lips and kisses are near any of your mucus membranes (any opening of your body), you can take their germs and the germs they get from other people into your body, and they become a part of you.

A lot of us grow up with notions of sexual intimacy being an emotional experience. But if you look at how a lot of music videos and TV and movies talk about and show sexual situations, it's sometimes treated like it's no big deal. Women are sometimes depicted as acting aggressively in sexual situations and it's becoming more commonplace for the media to show women as emotionally separated from sexual intimacy. What's absolutely true is that being sexually intimate has a lot of impact on humans, especially on females. Remember all of the hormones we talked about in the earlier chapters? Those are supercharged when we have sex. Even though being sexual is enjoyable, it does change a relationship when we're sexual with someone. Young people especially are not necessarily prepared to deal with some of the feelings that can come up when we have sexual relations with someone. Sometimes we may feel guilty, and sometimes we may feel it wasn't what we expected, and sometimes it can even feel like the other person didn't treat us the way we wanted to be treated.

It's important to acknowledge that having sex is a special thing, and it is a very big deal. Sex is very significant, and most people you talk to who have a lot of experience in life will tell you that sex is best when it's emotionally connected, not just when you do it as a purely physical act because it feels like the thing to do at the moment or because you think everyone else is doing it.

At the same time, although sex is very important, you shouldn't be afraid of it. Although many religious traditions have very strong opinions about sex for good reasons, and although many parents take the idea of their daughters' sexual activity very seriously—as they should—sex is not evil. It can be a beautiful way to connect with someone, and I can tell you from personal experience that the most meaningful, awesome sex comes from being in a solid, healthy relationship that involves a lot of trust, a lot of communication about everyone's needs and a lot of tenderness and fun.

HOW TO BE SMART ABOUT IT: I'm going to come right out and tell you that your body is awesome. Your body is made to feel good, and it's made to make babies if you want to do that someday. You deserve to feel good, and you also deserve to feel safe. You get to decide who touches you where and when, and no one should ever make you feel bad for not wanting to be touched. Anyone who tries to pressure you into doing things you aren't ready to do should be avoided, and you should talk to someone you trust if that person is persistent and won't leave you alone. Sexuality is a super-personal thing, and it's not anybody's decision but yours what you do, when you do it and how you do it.

Consent

It is your right to control your body. No matter what, there is no situation where anyone has the right to think they can touch you or kiss you or have sex with you if you don't want to. The notion of consent has nothing to do with the clothes you wear, the way you flirt with someone or even agreeing to be treated to dinner. Consent means you've given someone permission to do something. Sex must be agreed on by both people involved, and if you change your mind at any point during a date regarding how far you want to go, that's okay. You are allowed to change your mind, and that needs to be respected. If someone resists your limits, it is important to leave the situation immediately, even if you feel like you might be hurting their feelings or you worry that they will start rumors about you. A lot of messages we get from music and TV tell us that it's a woman's job to please men; it's not. Our job is to do things that make us happy and protect ourselves from experiences that we aren't interested in or ready for. "No" always means "no," without exception. Avoiding situations where there is alcohol (which can make decision making really confusing, especially for underage drinkers) is a great rule in general when you're out on a date, as is always having access to a ride home. Plan ahead for dates and be prepared. And know that you're in control of your body and your decisions.

If someone is sexually abusing you, RAINN (Rape, Abuse & Incest National Network) can help you figure out what to do: rainn.org.

If you do decide to be sexually active, you have to know that condoms should be used anytime fluid can enter your body from someone's genitals. Condoms prevent you from getting diseases that come from other people's body fluids and can stay with you and affect your life forever. A proper understanding of the ways to prevent pregnancy and sexually transmitted diseases is super important. You can talk to your family doctor, parents or another trusted adult about it. There are some diseases you can get from having sexual relations that never go away. They can affect your ability to have babies later in life. It's scary. And being careful about who you have sex with is very important. Like I said before, people you meet online and know very little about are not safe people just because they say they are. Making smart choices now can have an effect on the rest of your life.

As for pregnancy, no one wants to think that they might get pregnant if they decide to have sex in high school or middle school. But here's the bottom line, and I'm going to be very clear about it: *having sex is what makes you get pregnant.* Condoms are very effective against pregnancy if they are used correctly. There are other ways to prevent pregnancy, and there are advantages and disadvantages to all of them. And there are people who think if you just have sex for a little time, then you won't get pregnant—that's not safe. If you don't want to get pregnant, the best way to do that is to not let semen get into your vagina. Semen is what comes out of the penis and carries the cells that, when they meet with an egg cell, make a baby. Period.

Contraception

The choice to have sex is a personal one, and the decision about how to not get pregnant is also personal. Because of the way the male and female bodies work, contraception typically consists of finding ways to stop an egg from meeting sperm. As I stated above, the only way to make sure you don't get pregnant is pretty clear, but here are the most common types of contraception. Keep in mind that *contraception has to be used correctly in order for it to work* as well as it can, and no contraception is 100 percent sure to not let you get pregnant. Also know that some sperm can also be released before ejaculation, so the "withdrawal/pull-out" method is not a reliable form of contraception.

1. **Condoms.** A condom fits over the penis to catch the sperm so they don't get into your vagina. When used correctly,

condoms are a very reliable form of birth control. Most condoms are made of latex, and you usually need to use a lubricant with a condom so that the latex doesn't feel uncomfortable. Condoms protect from sexually transmitted diseases by creating a barrier between two bodies; this is something that only condoms provide.

2. **The Pill.** A birth control pill is prescribed by a doctor, and it needs to be taken every day in order for it to work. The Pill is made up of hormones that stop the ovaries from sending eggs into the fallopian tubes. The hormones in the Pill are powerful, and your body may react with sore breasts and some weight gain, and some women feel a bit more moody and emotional than usual during their periods when they are on the Pill. Sometimes the Pill is prescribed for girls with menstrual cramps and mood swings but there are many ways to manage these things without the side effects of the Pill. Talking to your doctor or another woman you trust is important; don't be afraid to ask a lot of questions and make a decision you are comfortable with.

3. **Hormonal patch and hormonal rings.** Patches are like Band-Aids that contain the same kinds of hormones that are in the Pill. A patch has to be placed and removed at set times or it doesn't work. The hormonal ring is inserted into the vagina and stays there securely. Like a tampon, if it's in right, you don't feel it. The way the hormones are delivered for both of these methods tends to lead to fewer side effects than the Pill.

4. **Other birth control: IUD, shots, sterilization.** These are more invasive and complicated methods of birth control, which are typically not recommended for teenagers. Some women have an Intra-Uterine-Device (IUD) implanted in their uterus. It can be removed by a doctor whenever you

want. Some IUDs release hormones into the body, while others don't. IUDs disrupt the ability of eggs and sperm to make an embryo. Another method of birth control is hormonal injections, which stop the release of eggs. Finally, when you are sure that you don't ever want to have babies, there is a procedure you can have that "seals" the fallopian tubes so that the egg and sperm can't come together anymore.

Late Bloomers

Did anyone read this chapter and think, *What is she talking about?!* Or, *Eeeww! I don't want to talk about this stuff!* Or maybe, *I don't want to think about sex, and I don't even want to think about going on a date!* If so, that's totally fine! Everyone matures at a different pace, and the way you are is exactly the way you are supposed to be.

I don't even know if I could have gotten through this chapter when I was your age, and I might have had to wait until after high school to read it! You see, I was a late bloomer. Like, a super late bloomer.

I developed late; I was really short, and my body didn't get curves until I was about 16. I didn't start my menstrual cycle until late in high school. I was not interested in dating, and as I shared before, I had my first kiss when I was acting in a TV show when I was 14. I didn't have my first real boyfriend until I was 17, and I never "casually" dated. I never hooked up with guys at camp or at school; I have had only long-term relationships, and I believe very strongly in having one committed partner at a time.

You might be thinking I have no clue what dating is like or that I have no right to comment on it since I was a clueless teenager. But here's the thing: I didn't engage in that stuff because I wasn't ready, and that's okay. I was really freaked out when I learned about the diseases you can get from fooling around, and to be honest, I found a lot of guys my age kind of lame. I wasn't interested in any of them, except for Mischa, who barely knew I even existed.

The truth is, being a late bloomer turned out to be a good thing for me. The fact that I was left out of a lot of jokes and conversations because I couldn't relate didn't end up affecting me much in the long run. I have never found someone who hooked up with a lot of people who felt it made them better equipped to have a healthy relationship or marriage later in life—it was just a different path to getting there. One path isn't necessarily better than the other or a better predictor of your success in relationships or in the bedroom. Keep that in mind when people say things like, "If you want to learn how to be a good kisser, you need a lot of practice," because that's simply not true. And that's also the case for a lot of things people will say, such as, "The only way to be a good lover is to practice a lot." It's also not true. Being a good lover and partner is about being in touch with your feelings and your needs, and wanting to be there for someone you care about and have strong feelings for. You get to take your time with how fast or slow that happens. If you're with someone you don't trust or someone you are just not comfortable with, that's a signal something isn't right. Slow down and don't rush into anything.

I know that being a late bloomer saved me from a lot of the drama and heartache that can come from having lots of relationships, but people who experienced a lot of relationships can learn a lot from them, and that's fine, too. For me, as a very sensitive and vulnerable person, the brief experiences I've had with the ups and downs of trying to get people to like me and date me and then feeling let down and rejected if they didn't was enough to turn me off from pursuing it more. I spent a lot of time in middle school and high school studying, playing and listening to music and writing letters to friends. I liked reading and writing poetry, and while I sometimes felt lonely, looking back, I spent time learning the things I like and things I don't like, and I wouldn't change my being a late bloomer for anything. For all of the late bloomers out there who might feel they are missing out on something: it may seem like you are, but trust me, everyone progresses in their own way in their own time, and it's important to listen to your intuition. We all get there eventually and it is very important for you to honor your intuition and to always go at your own pace.

If it feels wrong to make out with someone or hook up with them or to have sex, listen to your inner voice! I went to a dance through a Jewish organization when I was about 15, and some guy tried to stick his tongue in my mouth while we were slow dancing. I pulled away abruptly and said, "I'm not ready for that!" I felt bad for the guy because I wasn't very suave about it. I felt like such a dork, and it makes me embarrassed to think about it to this day, but I was taught to respect my body and my space and the decision to stop him when I knew I wasn't ready for that. If it feels yucky or icky or scary to move forward with someone physically or sexually, that's your brain and body's way of telling you it's a good idea to back off and give yourself some space. You'll be glad you did in the long run.

On *The Big Bang Theory*, I play a late bloomer who didn't have sex until she was well into her adult life. My character, Amy, had been dating Sheldon for years before he was ready to have a first kiss with her, and she had never been kissed before! Amy decided that being patient and waiting until Sheldon was ready was important, and it was an indication of her love for him. Sheldon, in the 9th season of our show, decided to make his birthday gift for Amy the gift of sexual intimacy. Amy was really shocked, and she and Sheldon were both nervous when they decided to make their relationship sexual. Sheldon said a sweet thing. He said, "We can find out together." And they did.

We all figure it out one way or the other. The thing I've treasured most about my late-bloomer journey is being able to take a lot of time to make decisions and to weigh whether my choices felt right or not. I used to feel ashamed that I was such a late bloomer, but now I embrace it, and I get to experience a lot of beauty and joy and love in ways I never imagined I could when I was a shy, awkward girl.

◆ ◆ ◆

Wrapping Up

Understanding emotions and feeling things deeply is such an important part of Girling Up. Learning how your emotions and feelings impact other people is what will make you a wonderful friend, daughter, sibling, girlfriend and wife, if that's what you choose to be. It's hard to always make conscious and thoughtful decisions about how we give our heart away and how to use our bodies to express affection. Thinking about things the way this chapter has, I hope, helped you think about them is a great start to making confident and healthy decisions as you Girl Up.

Know that your feelings and your heart and your body are wonderful vessels for communicating some of the most profound and life-changing things we get to experience as humans. Learn about your body, trust your gut and don't ever be afraid to put the brakes on anything that doesn't feel right. That's the best gift you can give yourself as well as those you choose to be close to.

five

• HOW WE COPE •

The transition from girl to young woman, which I've called Girling Up, is an incredibly exciting one. Being alive at this time in history is so spectacular, and there is so much to celebrate.

But is life all about spectacular celebration? Is everything always wonderful and smooth sailing?

When I watch TV or go to the movies, or when I look on social media, I see a lot of spectacular things and super-happy people. I see people with smiling families, adorable pets, beautiful houses, supportive friends, loving relationships and what often looks like perfect lives. The things people post show a world of joy and success. But that's not what life is always like. Bad things happen. We get sad. Situations come up that we don't always know how to handle. And sometimes it can feel like, if our life isn't the way other people's lives look, there's something wrong with us.

Psychologists and sociologists are experts on why and how people do the things they do, and they have defined the following things as the most challenging and prone to make us feel stressed out:

1. Moving to a new house or apartment
2. Death of someone close to you
3. Divorce in your family
4. Problems with money in your family

What are some other things that can be stressful?

1. Breaking up with someone or having a fight with a close friend
2. Having romantic feelings for someone who doesn't feel them back
3. Being teased or bullied for being different
4. Pressure from parents to do well in school
5. Difficult relationships with siblings or other family members
6. Having a family member in the military
7. Hearing in the news about some of the stuff that's going on in the world

Even though these things are not as stressful as death or divorce or moving or money problems, they are still stressful, and they can affect us in big ways.

◆　◆　◆

What Is Stress?

So what exactly is stress? What does it do, and how does it change us?

The word is sometimes used to describe the pressure of, say, a bowling ball resting on a flimsy table; the table is under the stress of a super-heavy weight—that's physical stress. Emotional stress is not so different. It's the pressure we feel when we've been put in a really difficult, challenging situation. Stress affects the body and the brain, and stress can also affect the way we deal with people around us and the things we have to do, even if they have nothing to do with the actual thing that's stressing us out. So being stressed about one thing can turn into being stressed about a lot of things; in that way, stress kind of grows.

Stressful situations can be physical, such as being approached by an angry dog who looks like he's ready to attack you. Or stressful things can affect feelings and behavior, such as the loss of someone we love. When we are challenged physically, our brains get the message that something needs attention and that we have to do something about it, usually right away. There is a part of the brain called the amygdala that is responsible for us feeling fear and knowing what to do when things are scary. So if we are approached by an angry dog, this triggers the amygdala, and it says, "Whoa! Holy moly: DOG!" The next thing that happens is our amygdala starts communicating with the rest of the brain to initiate things that will help us protect ourselves from this threat.

If you've ever heard of the expression "fight or flight," you have an idea of what your brain is responsible for when it feels it's under attack. The body sends extra blood to our muscles so that we can either use our muscles to defend ourselves (if we choose to fight) or to run away (if we choose to engage in getting the heck out of there, also known as flight). Our brains send information to our hearts to pump extra blood, and this raises our heart rate and blood pressure. Our brains also send hormones into our blood, such as adrenaline for energy and endorphins to give us the confidence to protect ourselves. These hormones and the increase in blood flow to the heart explain the fluttery feeling you might have experienced if you've ever been scared or threatened. (It also happens when you see someone you have a crush on, but for slightly different reasons!)

So our bodies perceive stressful things as threats that need to be fixed one of two ways: by fighting or by running away.

Here's a diagram of some parts of our brain and what they do.

But what about emotional stress? How does that get handled by our brains and bodies?

To the brain, emotional stress is actually not that different from physical threat. When we encounter an emotionally threatening or stressful situation, the brain gets a message: stressful situation happening! And even though emotional or psychological stress may be

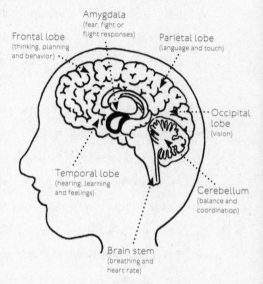

Amygdala
(fear, fight or flight responses)

Frontal lobe
(thinking, planning and behavior)

Parietal lobe
(language and touch)

Occipital lobe
(vision)

Temporal lobe
(hearing, learning and feelings)

Cerebellum
(balance and coordination)

Brain stem
(breathing and heart rate)

different from a one-time event such as an angry dog approaching you, the brain still starts sending out hormonal messengers into the body to start protecting us from what the brain interprets as an emotional attack.

The difference when we experience an emotionally or psychologically stressful situation is caused by the fact that the brain keeps trying to support us for however long a situation is happening. For example, if you have a family member in the military, you are going to have some strong feelings about it. You might feel sad, and you might miss that person. You might be scared for their safety, and you may take an extra interest in the news so you can see if the place they are stationed is ever mentioned. These are all real concerns, and they are stressful for sure. Your brain will be on alert for a long period of time—until your loved one comes back from the military. It's not a one-time thing; it's a prolonged stress.

The amazing thing about the brain is that it can provide support in ways that will help you be able to function at school and at home so that kind of prolonged stress won't take over your whole life. The brain can process more than one thing at a time! The way it does this is by allowing us to be distracted, even for short periods of time, by tasks at school, parties we're invited to and daily things that need to get done such as chores and being a productive part of activities. In this way, we can have something we are stressed about going on while we also can enjoy things and continue our lives even with this constant stressful thing going on in the back of our minds, as it were.

Here's the catch, though: everyone's brain works slightly differently, and everyone reacts differently to stress. So for some people, the death of a family pet might make them feel devastated for a week but then they can get back to "normal" life and mostly feel unaffected by it. They might still miss their pet and get sad from time to time, but for the most part, they will feel fine about it after a short time. This is totally normal. For other people, the death of a pet might stay with them for a long time. They may feel sad for months. This is also totally normal.

The differences in how people react to stress depend on a lot of things. Genetics and what kinds of personality features you inherited from your parents come into play. So do the environment and how your family taught you to understand feelings and what to do with them. Your reactions also depend on things you have control over, such as emotional skills you can use to help you get through hard times. In addition, stress is cumulative, which means when stresses happen, they add up, especially if you didn't work through previous stresses completely. So stressors can pile on top of each other and produce even bigger reactions than we might have had if we were only dealing with one stressful thing at a time.

What Does Emotional Stress Look Like?

If we are in a stressful situation that is not about fight or flight but is instead about something emotional, here are some of the things that we may experience, especially if the stress continues for a while or if we are having a hard time understanding how to feel about the stress.

1. **Changes to our bodies:**
   - We may lose or gain weight. Some people eat more than they usually do when they are stressed; some people find it hard to eat.
   - We may feel achy or tired a lot.
   - We may find it hard to concentrate or think straight.

2. **Sad feelings:**
   - We may feel hopeless and lose interest in things we previously had interest in, such as hobbies or friends or activities at school.
   - Life may seem "blah," and we may feel like just hanging around rather than going out and doing things. Even getting out of bed or getting dressed can feel like a chore. It may even feel as if we are trudging through mud just to get up and get going.

3. **Angry feelings:**
   - We may feel irritable, short-tempered and angry, sometimes for no apparent reason or out of the blue.
   - We may feel like hurting ourselves or other people, or throwing or even breaking things.

These symptoms and feelings are the body and brain's reactions to stress. Over time, these feelings can get stronger and stronger, and unless we find ways to deal with them, we can do damage to our bodies, our brains and our relationships.

When Sadness Becomes Depression

Sudden weight loss or weight gain accompanied by prolonged feelings of tiredness, hopelessness and losing interest in things we previously loved doing can also occur in a condition called depression. Depression is different from sadness, and if you are feeling sad and hopeless for longer than 2 weeks, talk to a doctor, parent or trusted teacher about it and tell them you think you may be depressed. In addition, if you find you are feeling intensely sad with nothing stressful going on, talk to someone. There is help for you, and it's very important to talk to someone early on in depression so you can get the help you need before it escalates into a bigger problem that may be harder for you to handle.

Coping

One of the most important things to understand about emotional stress is that there are ways to make it better, even if it seems like nothing will make it better. It's called *coping*. Sadly, a lot of us don't know how to cope in healthy ways. Instead, we may turn to unhealthy ways to cope to try to make us feel better.

ANGER

Stress can make people feel angry, even if there's nothing that anger can do to make the stress go away. Anger can be a useful emotion when it signals to us that something is wrong or upsetting, and it can motivate us to do things to change the situation. The thing about emotional stress is that it doesn't always go away if we get angry at it. And sometimes people take their anger out on others by yelling at them, hitting them or being mean to them with words and actions. This does not lessen the source of the stress, and in fact it can lead to more stress, even if it makes the angry person feel better in the moment. Being abusive or taking out your anger on others actually triggers more stress in your body over time, so if you see yourself doing this when you're stressed out, take a deep breath and try to come up with some other ways to cope with what's upsetting you. Talking to someone you trust can help a lot, and most everyone has had angry feelings, so know that you're not alone.

When Anger Becomes Violence

It is never okay for someone to hit you or hurt you because they are angry, even if they tell you it's your fault and even if they are your parent or sibling or friend. If you feel scared in your home or in any relationship, you deserve to speak up and be protected.

If you're in any sort of abusive situation, or know someone who is, don't hesitate to ask for help. Talk to a trusted adult, or use some of these resources:

- If you're facing abuse at home, you can get help from the National Domestic Violence Hotline at TheHotline.org.
- And if you're in a relationship that is abusive in any way, Loveisrespect offers empowering resources at loveisrespect.org.

DISTRACTION

Sometimes people drink or use drugs or even zone out in front of the TV to avoid dealing with the emotions stressful situations can bring up. These distractions work for the moment, but they don't actually do anything to help us move past those hard feelings. Over time, alcohol and drugs can become a crutch and a danger to your health, and they contribute to making a lot of choices that ultimately can impact your life in damaging ways. Zoning out in front of the TV is sometimes okay to give us a break from stressing out, but this kind of distracting ourselves is not a long-term solution to understanding our feelings and doing productive things with them.

When Someone's Drinking or Drug Use Becomes a Problem

Drugs and alcohol cause significant changes to the brain, even the first time you use them. These substances activate chemicals in your brain that make you feel certain things by hijacking your brain's normal operations. When on drugs or when drinking, some people think they are super strong or super confident, or they develop a craving for feeling 'zoned out.' Over time, the brain gets addicted to drugs and alcohol, which means that you start craving them even if you think you can do without them or would like to not need them. Addiction can make you disoriented and fixated on planning ways to get that drug or alcohol into your body. Addicts often make incredibly poor decisions, which can damage relationships, physical well-being and mental health. If you feel you can't cope without drugs or alcohol, get help as soon as possible. Alcoholics Anonymous is a widely regarded resource for addiction: www.aa.org. If someone in your home or your life drinks or uses drugs in a way that makes you uncomfortable or scares you, you don't have to handle it on your own. Talk to someone you can trust, or reach out to Alateen, an anonymous organization that was created to help people living with the effects of someone else's drinking (or drug use). Their website is www.al-anon.alateen.org.

HEALTHY COPING

If anger, drinking, drugs and watching tons of TV are unhealthy ways to cope with stress, what are some examples of healthy ways people cope?

Fortunately, there are a lot of things we can do. The first thing that is helpful is learning to trust other people in a stressful time by reaching out and not isolating yourself if you're struggling. Stress and sadness thrive in darkness, and we have to bring them out of the darkness of our brains and hearts to shed light on them. Relying on other people for help and support is not something that comes naturally to all of us. But keep in mind that for all of human history, people have lived in communities, because it allows them to know each other and help support each other. Community means there are people around you who know you and your family, and who can be there in a way that works for you. Maybe you've experienced this in your community if there was a natural disaster such as a fire or a flood or an earthquake or tornado. Have you noticed how people come together to help each other? And not just firefighters and the police—community members are supposed to help each other, and they often do.

Don't be afraid to share your feelings with others. If you don't feel comfortable talking to someone in your family, find a school counselor or teacher you can trust. Sometimes the parents of a friend might feel like good people to talk to, and that's a safe place to start as well.

Another way to cope with stress is by participating in events where people already congregate. Have your parents ever tried to make you go to a religious service when you're going through a rough time? It can feel awkward, and it can make you feel vulnerable, and that can be uncomfortable, but it can also help a lot. The reason it's encouraged is because it's good for us to be around people so that we don't have to go through tough stuff alone. By doing this, we start to learn more about what and who can be helpful to us.

Over thousands of years, religions have created a lot of rituals that can help in times of stress. So even if organized religion isn't something you think you want to be a part of, there are aspects that we can apply to our lives even outside of a formal religious setting which can help in times of stress.

Here are some of the benefits people have found from being a part of a religious community that comes together in stressful times.

1. **Help.** Have you ever been away at camp and felt homesick? Or have you ever been upset about something at school? Chances are, you got a taste for what community can do for you when you needed it in these situations. Community helps you feel not alone. Having people around can distract you in healthy ways and help you understand your feelings in a larger context than if you tried to figure it all out on your own. In communities that are close, when someone in the family dies or when a new baby is born, people from the community show up right away with food and help arrange for taking care of the small kids so that the adults can talk and work out details without worrying about making food and caring for children. It really helps to have people around when stressful things happen, and communities make that possible. (Of course there are nonreligious communities and activities that can make this kind of connection happen as well,

but the structure of religious organizations
causes people to congregate regularly and get to
know each other on a more regular basis.)

2. **Focus.** Sometimes when we are stressed, it feels
like the stressful thing is all we can think about.
Gathering together in a peaceful setting such as a
church or synagogue or mosque forces us to shake
up our thoughts and try something new in our
brains. It forces us to focus on something other
than the stressful situation. This kind of focus
helps the brain start to get on board with shifting
the stressful dynamics that are happening. The
sadness or frustration or despair or anger we may
be feeling can be disrupted—even for a short
time—and this starts a pattern in your brain of
working things out.

3. **Prayer.** Prayer is a form of talking things out.
Even if you don't believe in God, you can benefit
from having quiet time to talk out—even in your
head—what's going on. Prayer can look like a lot
of different things, and it can often feel like a lot
of thanking God for stuff. This might not seem
like a logical thing to participate in if something
horrible is going on, but the process of prayer
allows us to find places in our brains and hearts
where we can be grateful for things that are okay

even when there are so many things that may not feel okay. Shifting our thinking from "everything stinks" to "certain things stink, but certain things don't" is a really good start toward helping your brain get you out of a stress funk.

4. **Meditation.** Many religious traditions incorporate meditation into their practice, especially the Eastern religions. If you think of prayer as talking, meditation is just listening. There are many ways to meditate, but the basic idea is to stop what you're doing and find a quiet space to be with your thoughts and to breathe slowly and deeply. There are ways to meditate that involve listening to someone talking you through a breathing exercise, and there are ways to meditate where you just sit and try to not let thoughts linger in your mind. There are even ways to meditate while walking; you walk very slowly and think really hard about each step you take—kind of cool, right? And what's even cooler is that scientific research has shown that meditating improves immune system functioning and is linked to less anxiety and depression, so meditating is really a win-win choice for healthy coping! (See box on page 140.)

Another way to deal with stress in a healthy way is by doing something physical and productive, as opposed to bottling up angry feelings or using violence or aggression. The energy you expend through practicing, training and competing makes for a great release of stress and tension. Athletes sometimes talk about being "in the zone" when they are training, and you sometimes feel a "high" when your body really starts moving. For those of us with a tendency to be stressed out or angry or tense, being physical in sports is a healthy and safe way to burn off excess energy and emotions. Sometimes when I'm really stressed out, I will take a brisk walk or a jog, and I can literally feel the negative feelings leaving my body with every step I take. Being an athlete is not without its stresses, but the act of being physical is a great way to burn off energy no matter how you do it.

Using healthy ways to get the brain out of its initial stressful upset encourages it to send out calming signals to the body. Happy hormones get woken up that may have been sleeping because of the stress. Once the brain starts to send out those happy hormones, like serotonin and dopamine, it starts to chip away at all of the sad stuff floating around the brain and body. And the neat thing about these happy hormones is that the brain is kind of addicted to them: once it has a taste of feeling a little bit better, it can start building you up to help you feel better for longer and longer periods of time.

COPING ON OUR OWN

Sometimes being around people in a community when we're going through a hard time can feel like it makes things worse. It's completely normal to want to be alone sometimes, and we're all entitled to some alone time all of the time, and especially when we're struggling. Alone time can actually be a very important part of learning to cope with stress, so it's important to make the most of it, especially if we don't have an opportunity to be part of a community or a religion because of where we live or circumstances that are not in our control.

So how can we bring healthy coping techniques into our life if we don't have a community around or if we don't want to be with other people? It's actually easier than you think, and it often doesn't even have to involve leaving your bedroom. In many cases, it involves using things you have around your house and inside of you already.

A general principle for using your own techniques to cope with stress and hard stuff is to become familiar and comfortable with the notion of mindfulness in everything that you do, like we talked about with eating. Mindfulness means appreciating what's going on and slowing down enough to acknowledge the changes that are happening all of the time. For each of the following examples, being aware of what's right in front of you and appreciative of what you can identify as positive will be a great start.

Here are some of my favorite things to do alone (or with a buddy if you want!) to cope with stress.

1. **Shake things up.** Any time you do something
    outside of your normal routine, your brain gets a
    wake-up call. It's like you're saying to a stressed-
    out brain, "Hey there! Let's try something
    different!" Even small changes to your routine can
    be a good place to start in working on stress. Go
    someplace you've never gone. Walk a different way
    to homeroom. Explore a park you've never been
    to. Talk to a kid in school you've never talked to.
    Try a different food for lunch. Change your nail
    polish color. Get a haircut (ask your parents first!).
    Rearranging the stuff in my room was something
    I used to love to do; I would change the dolls and
    books I had on my shelves or the posters on my
    walls just to do something different. Any change
    can be good change, even small changes!

2. **Shift your perspective.** Positive thinking and
    "self-talk" might sound silly, but you'd be surprised
    how much scientific evidence there is that it actually
    works to improve our mood and decrease the
    negative impacts of stress. Inspirational quotes can be
    found all over the internet, and when you find one
    that inspires you, copy it and post it on your mirror
    or inside of your locker. (Some of my favorites can be
    found at the end of this section.) Remind yourself
    as much as you need to that *no one's life is perfect*.

Everyone has challenges. If you're feeling down, know that life gets better. You won't always feel sad, even if you feel sad right now. Flood your brain with positivity.

3. **Nature.** The wonders of the natural world have been celebrated for all of human history. The oceans, lakes and streams; mountains, hills and valleys; the clouds and the sky and all of the wonders of the natural world have inspired poets, painters, rabbis, priests, imams and monks for as long as humans have walked this earth. Nature has a way of making us feel very small (There are so many stars in the sky and planets out there, how can I even matter?!) and also very big (This universe is so huge, and I get to be a part of it—wow!). Try to bring even small doses of nature into your day. Look at a flower that you normally might walk right by. Admire the way a tree arches up to the sky, seeking nourishment from the glorious giant hot ball of gas that is the sun. Follow a leaf as the wind carries it along a street. Take a second to appreciate that all of these things are not created by humans, but rather are the product of the glory of the scientific world and natural events of the universe. It should make you feel both humble and empowered, and it can have a super-positive effect on your overall mood and attitude.

4. **Move your body.** Research has shown that walking even for 15 minutes around the block can really boost your mood if you make a habit of it. Increasing the circulation of blood and oxygen by moving your body around and getting your heart pumping a few times a week elevates your happy hormone levels and trains your body to crave more of them. Dancing is a great way to move, and music can make for fun that won't feel like a chore at all. If walking and dancing aren't your thing, try something new like a sport you've been thinking about but never had the courage to pursue. If you don't like it, find something else that works. The key is to move your body any way that strikes your fancy.

5. **Art.** Making art and learning about art are great ways to expand your mind and feed your creative brain, which can boost your mood tremendously. Painting, drawing or even working with clay can be very therapeutic. I like listening to music that speaks to how I'm feeling, especially when I'm down. I also like to play the piano, because it feels like my emotions get more manageable when I can play them out. Sometimes I'll write in a journal about my feelings, and I sometimes write poetry because I like the challenge of finding words that

rhyme to match my mood. In middle school, poetry was a really safe place for me to share my feelings for Mischa, the boy I had a big crush on but who barely knew I existed. As a grown-up, I make collages out of pictures and trinkets and fabric and anything I have around the house, because being creative is soothing, and making something out of nothing gives the brain a real boost.

6. **Meditate.** As I mentioned above, meditation is something you can do on your own any time of day or night with little or no preparation needed. A basic sitting meditation practice starts like this: sit in a chair with a straight back. You want to be comfortable, and there shouldn't be any strain on your back or neck. (You can also lie down to meditate, but the key is to not fall asleep, and when I lie down, I tend to want to go right to sleep!) Close your eyes gently and become aware of your breath. Breathe slowly and deeply and try to just focus on being aware of your breath. It's totally normal to have other thoughts come into your head, like what's for dinner or what homework you have to do or how cute what's-his-name looked in gym today. Even with a lot of meditation experience, I still think about what's for dinner and the toilets that have to be

scrubbed and also sometimes cute boys when I
meditate; trust me, it's hard not to think about
other things! The main goal is to not feel bad
about your mind wandering. Just let the thoughts
pass on by without you beating yourself up over
not being able to focus. The goal is to not have
as many thoughts come and for them not to stay
very long. Keep in mind that people practice their
whole lives to perfect this, and monks in some
religions literally spend their entire lives mastering
meditation; it's not easy! Just like you have to
build up a muscle when you want to learn a new
sport or lift weights, meditation takes practice
and the use of the most powerful "muscle" in your
body: your brain!

7. **Simple pleasures.** There are simple things that
make me happy when I'm feeling down or stressed
out, like having a cup of tea or writing a letter
or email to a friend I haven't spoken to in a while
but miss a lot. Or taking a bath and using my
favorite body lotion, which smells really good, is
something I love—maybe it's because I grew up
with four people sharing one bathroom in our
house until I was 15, so I really enjoy alone time
in a bath without being rushed! If you promise not
to laugh, I'll share with you one of my silliest but

most favorite simple pleasures . . . I have a folder
in my desk of pictures I love of cute animals. It's
mostly monkey and cat pictures I've collected
from magazines. I look at these pictures when I
need a smile. I know it's silly, but it's something
that costs no money, doesn't require a membership
to a club and takes just a second. It really does
work wonders for me to peek at a monkey wearing
glasses and a top hat, and I know that my brain
is thanking me for that shot of cuteness. Simple
pleasures can go a long way. It's important to find
what those simple pleasures are for you.

Some Inspirational Quotes

"A woman is like a tea bag; you never know how strong it is
until it's in hot water."—*Eleanor Roosevelt*

"There are two ways of spreading light: to be the candle or the
mirror that reflects it."—*Edith Wharton*

"The best and most beautiful things in the world cannot be seen or
even touched—they must be felt with the heart."—*Helen Keller*

"Remember that sometimes not getting what you want
is a wonderful stroke of luck."—*Dalai Lama*

"Make the most of yourself by fanning the tiny, inner sparks
of possibility into flames of achievement."—*Golda Meir*

"Take the first step in faith. You don't have to see the whole
staircase, just take the first step."—*Dr. Martin Luther King, Jr.*

Meditation for Inspiration

Here are some meditations you can do on your own once you are
breathing slowly and deeply. Even doing these for 5 minutes can make
a big difference in how your body reacts to stress on a daily basis.

1. **Locate the breath.** Concentrate on where you feel the
   breath as you breathe. Focus on the breath starting in your
   belly, and try to feel your belly expanding as it takes in air like
   a big balloon would. Breathe in through your nose and feel
   how the air tickles the outside of your nostrils. Let the breath
   out through your mouth slowly and feel the air as it moves past
   your lips. Keep doing that, taking slow and deep breaths. The
   goal is to be still with the breath and not force it at all.

2. **In and out.** Try counting breaths and try to let that number
   be the only thing in your head. So breathe in and think, *In one,*
   and then when you breathe out, think, *Out one,* and then take
   a second deep breath and think, *In two,* and then exhale and
   think, *Out two,* and so on. How many breaths can you count
   to without losing concentration? If you get distracted, don't
   stress out! Just start again and try to get to a higher number.

3. **How long can you breathe?** Slow your breathing down and take long, deep breaths without feeling like you are holding anything in. Count how long it takes to take a full breath in and then count how long it takes to breathe it all out. Usually the exhale is longer than the inhale. Can you breathe in for 5 seconds and then out for 7? Can you slow your breath down even more so that you breathe in for 6 seconds and out for 8? You shouldn't ever feel out of breath; the goal is to train your body to slow your breath down and to quiet your thoughts while you focus on the breath.

4. **Walk!** If you want to do a walking meditation, remember that you need to keep your eyes open! Go somewhere where you can take about 10 steps in a straight line. It should be a quiet place, like a hallway where people won't be walking around, or in a yard or a park. Lift one leg and start to take a step very slowly, so slowly that you need to balance on the leg that's supporting you while you move your foot as slowly as you can. It might feel funny at first, but the idea is to move with mindfulness and intention, and to be very deliberate. When your foot hits the ground, think about the heel hitting first, and then let your foot unfold onto the ground very slowly. Don't rush into lifting the other foot right away. Feel how your body adjusts to having two feet on the ground rather than just one and then shift your body to the front foot so you can slowly begin to lift your back foot. As you lift it, think about what it feels like to be aware of the back heel

coming up first, followed by the rest of the foot peeling off the ground. Lift slowly, once again balancing on the leg that's supporting you. Return to the start and breathe and feel the stability of being on both feet again. Now it's time to take your second step! It may also help to think of these words as you do this meditation: *lift* (for while you are slowly lifting your first foot), *place* (for when you place the foot down), *shift* (for when your body shifts to the front foot), *lift* (for when the back foot comes up) and *place* (for when it comes down again).

COPING WITH STRESS WITH THE HELP OF OTHERS

What about other ways to help with stress? When stress makes it difficult for you to do schoolwork or causes problems in relationships with your family and friends, it can be helpful to talk to your parent or a school counselor. You may also find that talking to a professional outside of your school who is trained to help you with your problems is helpful, too. One of the most revolutionary thinkers the world has ever seen was an Austrian man named Sigmund Freud who practiced neurology about a hundred years ago. Freud was the first person in history to describe how talking about problems out loud can lessen the weight and stress associated with them. Along with another doctor named Josef Breuer, Freud was the first to demonstrate and communicate how, when people form a relationship with someone who talks to them about their feelings and their struggles, they transfer some of their pain to that person, who can then help them work through it. This was the start of psychoanalysis, and it's the basis for what we now call psychotherapy or talk therapy.

Sometimes when we are under stress, we have a lot of problems with sleep, or we may have thoughts in our heads that won't go away. For some people, this kind of stress may lead them to do things repeatedly to help cope, and this can escalate and become disruptive to their lives. While psychotherapy is

also helpful for this, another kind of therapy that can be used for this kind of stress is called Cognitive Behavioral Therapy (CBT). CBT is designed as a more short-term, goal-oriented kind of therapy, where you have worksheets and "homework" to do and review with a therapist. CBT helps you understand your motivations for thinking the ways you think, while helping you find more productive ways to work through stress.

The scientific basis for talk therapy and CBT are the same: by behaving and thinking differently, we can change the chemistry of the brain so that we can make stress easier to deal with. There is no "magic" to therapy; the key is to be consistent with seeing a therapist and to ask questions when you don't agree with something or when you hear something that doesn't feel right to you. Most importantly, therapy can only work if you feel comfortable talking with the therapist. If you don't feel like you can share things with one therapist, ask to try another until you find one you can talk to openly and honestly.

A lot of therapy is not covered by insurance, and it can be expensive, but there are more and more free services popping up all over the country to allow more people to talk through their problems. Sometimes it can be scary to talk about feelings, but it really can help, and even a school counselor is a good place to start, since many are trained in basic therapy techniques.

Besides therapy, you've probably heard about medications that people can take to help them deal with stress. These are usually prescribed by a psychiatrist, which is a doctor who specializes in people's emotions and the medications that affect them, but some pediatricians prescribe them, too. While these medications can indeed encourage your brain to send out more happy hormones and help decrease the sad ones, they often have strong side effects and they are not always made for growing bodies. Medication is often used when other ways to cope with stress don't work, or when someone's reactions to stress are affecting their ability to handle school, relationships and the way they function every day. It's important to know that medication doesn't have to be a "forever" thing. Sometimes people use medications to get through a particular situation, but with time, things get better and we find other ways to cope that make the medications not necessary. Only you and your parents and a doctor can help decide what's best for your family, and often, when medication is prescribed, talk therapy can also be really helpful.

Wrapping Up

In case you think I'm just making all of this coping stuff up, I'm going to share something super personal with you. You may know me from TV, or your parents may have bought you this book because they know me from TV, but I'm a real person who has lived through a lot, and a lot of it has been stressful. My family didn't have a lot of money when I was a kid, and life wasn't easy for me. In addition to losing a lot of tears over crushes I had which were unrequited and the death of my childhood cats when I was in middle school, which many of us experience, I was very small for my age and I developed late, so I was teased a lot. I cried a lot and felt left out of many things my whole life, and I still feel that way as an adult sometimes. My family had a lot of secrets, and I felt scared a lot.

I got divorced several years ago and moved houses within the same year, which hits on two of the "most stressful things" listed at the start of this chapter. The same year, I was in a car accident that led to several major surgeries. The following year, my dad got sick and died, I went through a major, devastating breakup and my 13-year-old cat had to be put down. That's another bunch of big stressors, right?

The things that I've talked about in this chapter that you can do to cope with stress are things I've done myself, and they are things I still do in order to maintain my emotional and mental health. They also affect my physical health, since stress impacts the body as well.

Here's what I do:

- I take walks a few times a week.
- I try to get time in nature, even if it just means hugging a tree whenever I can.
- I go to synagogue and pray that I have patience with people and things that annoy me. I also pray that I'll have a better perspective on life when I need it.
- I practice deep breathing and try to meditate a few times a week, sitting in my bed and listening to the sounds around me, even if all I can hear is cars and my own messy thoughts.
- I force myself to be in social community settings at least once a week so that I don't isolate myself from people.
- I make lists of things to be grateful for every day, even if it's just a few things like being grateful for having clean water to drink and my cat who needs me.
- I play the piano and sing sad songs when I need to

be reminded that I'm not alone; there are musicians whose lyrics indicate that they have also experienced sadness, too. Listening to music with lyrics I can relate to helps me work through hard feelings.

- I go to therapy every week and talk about my feelings, even when it's hard and I don't want to.
- I follow a few accounts on Instagram that feature positive quotes, so that while I'm scrolling through my feed and looking at all of the people who seem to have a much more put-together life—or hairstyle or outfit—than I do, I can be reminded that I'm also okay just as I am. These quotes tell me that when things feel hard, I need to be patient and know that they will eventually pass with some hard work and more time.
- And don't forget my folder of pictures of cute monkeys and cats . . .

All of the things I do to cope may not feel like they are working right away, but with time and patience, they do help and they contribute to my overall well-being and mental and physical health in the long run. From one stressed-out person to another, I hope you will trust me and find ways to cope that bring you joy and peace.

six

• HOW WE MATTER •

We have been exploring a lot of the "nuts and bolts" of Girling Up so far: how our bodies grow, how we spend our time, how we learn, how we go about dating and socializing, how we cope with hard stuff . . . It seems like we've kind of covered it all. But there is another very important part of Girling Up, which involves thinking bigger about our lives and our decisions. Are there ways that the big and small things we do make an impact on others? Should they? I guess the basic underlying question is: do we matter in this world? If you already believe we matter, I agree with you, and I'm eager to think about ways to transform that belief into action that can have a bigger impact. And if you're on the fence about how much we matter, let's find ways to focus on how we can change that!

The decisions we make and the things we say and do can impact other people in very powerful ways, and part of the process of Girling Up is understanding how that happens and finding ways to make it a significant part of life. Finding out how we matter can help boost our confidence, increase our feelings of belonging and purpose and inspire others to make an impact, too.

When we think about how we matter, a big part of that involves seeing our life as more than just this very moment. What we do today and next week is important, but so is thinking about what will happen *after* today and next week. A combination of being present and also being realistic about what's not right in front of us is important as we continue Girling Up.

The Future

One of the ways we do this is to think really hard—even for just a little bit—about the future. And don't worry: I'm not talking about planning out the rest of your life right now. Even if we tried to, we couldn't know what was going to happen anyway! When I say we should think about the future, what I mean is this: it's not too early to start thinking about what you might want your life to look like when you are done Girling Up and become a grown-up girl.

Why is it important to think about this kind of stuff now? Because the choices we make now actually impact what our future will look like. And no, I'm not saying that the flavor of ice cream you choose tonight will have an impact on your future or that the note you realize you should not have passed in class today about that girl who you think is mean to you is going to come back and haunt you for the rest of your life. And I'm for sure not saying that skipping class last Thursday is going to negatively impact your chances of being able to own a house someday.

What I am saying is this: what you do now frames your life and your attitudes. So while chocolate or vanilla tonight may not matter, you know that what you put into your body over time does matter. And today's note about the mean girl may not matter, but the way we view other women and the way we choose to engage— or not—in gossip do matter. And last Thursday's class doesn't matter, but consistently choosing to miss class does matter.

You don't have to plan out the rest of your life today, tomorrow or next week. But it is a great idea to think about the future, because thinking about your future and talking it out with someone else is a great start to turning your future into whatever you can dream it to be!

After High School

Finishing high school is a huge accomplishment, and whenever you finish an accomplishment in life, the following question is bound to come up: what next?!

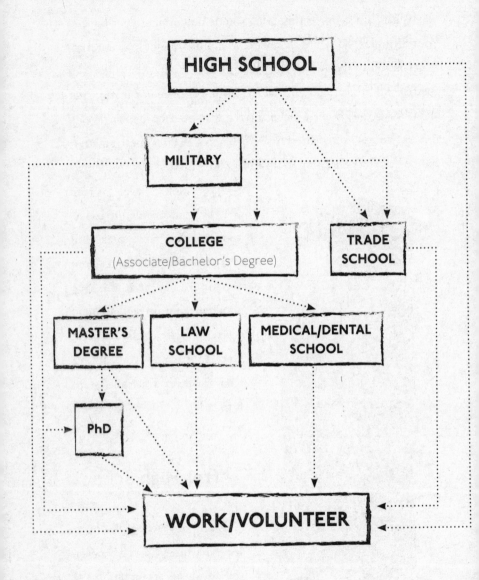

LIFESTYLE

One of the best exercises to do when you want to ponder the future is to think about what kind of life you see for yourself when you grow up.

For example, do you want to be a mom? Can you picture what that might be like? Once you get pregnant, your life changes dramatically, and for almost 10 months you are responsible for growing a baby. As your belly grows, there are more and more things you might find hard to do, and everything you eat and drink goes into your baby's developing body; it's a big responsibility! Giving birth is a natural event that can be a wonderful experience, but it should not be thought of as just another thing to do; it's a big deal to give birth and recover from labor.

Being a mom is the hardest job I've ever had, and I waited until I was almost 30 to have my first son; I had my second son a few years later. Some women have babies early in their lives, and in most cases, a young body can recover really well from birth and you can get back to "normal" quicker than if you're an older mom. Remember that, once you have kids, they are yours forever, and the rest of your life pretty much revolves around planning for their needs: feeding them, clothing them, making sure they go to school and do their homework and all of the stuff your parents do for you!

If you have kids, you can still have a career, but keep in mind that when you work, someone needs to be with your children! It's also your job to figure out child care and pay for their care while you are at work. Being a mom is a huge responsibility, and the more you prepare, the better off you'll be. Typically, that kind of preparation happens into your 20s, so take your time!

When you think about the future, where do you see yourself living? Would you like to stay in your hometown? Is being close to family something that is an important factor in your decision about where you might live after high school? If it isn't, what are some of the places in the country where you live that you can imagine moving to? Could you imagine living in another country? If you can't imagine living in another place, do you want to have a career that allows for a lot of travel? If so, there are many jobs that involve traveling, such as working for a hotel or tour company or even working as a dancer or singer on cruises and at resorts. If travel is something you can picture yourself doing, know that there are ways to make that part of your life.

Even though all of these decisions seem so far off, it's never too soon to start thinking about what you see your life looking like in just a handful of years. Letting your mind wander can sometimes be a really healthy exercise!

COLLEGE

While there are jobs you can get right out of high school such as in food service and retail or working in an office, many people choose to go to college because the degree you get when you go to college opens up a different pool of jobs, and it often sets you on a course to earn more money and have more experiences in the working world.

If you aren't ready or don't have the grades to enter a four-year college right away, starting at a community college is a good plan to consider. You can transfer your credits from the classes you take at a two-year college to a four-year one when you're ready, or you can earn an associate of arts degree (also known as an "AA"). There are advantages to community college: it gives you some time to adjust to the workload of college in a smaller setting, and since many basic courses at community college are essentially the same as at a larger college, you can save a lot of money by taking those classes closer to home (thus saving money on renting an apartment or moving into dorms, for example), where living may be less costly in general.

There are two main degrees you can get in a four-year college: a bachelor of arts or a bachelor of science degree, more commonly known as a "BA" or a "BS." BA degrees are in what's called the humanities, such as English, history, political science or communications. BA degrees can also be in one of the arts, such as drama, creative writing, painting, music or dance. Some people choose to get a BA degree focusing on another language, such as Spanish. In fact, you can get an entire degree based on studying Spanish and learning about any Spanish-speaking country in the world. You can even study abroad if you want to! Some schools also offer a bachelor of fine arts, or "BFA," which involves spending a lot of time in a studio making art or music or theater or creative writing.

Most people you encounter working in a nonmedical or

nonscientific field likely have BA degrees if they went to college. Even though BA degrees are based on the humanities subjects, almost every college you can get a BA degree from also educates you in the basic math and science that you'll need for general knowledge in your life and career. So whether you choose to be a preschool teacher or a manager of a clothing store or restaurant, or if you want to work in a lawyer's office or work for a website, a BA is a great start.

BS degrees are in the sciences, such as biology, chemistry, physics, engineering and, my personal favorite, neuroscience. Many people with BS degrees go on to medical or dental school so that they can be doctors or dentists. I went to graduate school to get a PhD in neuroscience after getting my BS degree, and people with PhDs typically teach in colleges and universities and do medical research.

MORE COLLEGE?!

Some people enter the workforce after their undergraduate degree is completed armed with their BA or BS degree. Others pursue more schooling to get a more advanced degree. People who want to get more education and a higher degree have to go to some sort of graduate school to get that degree. Graduate school is kind of like college after college, but with smaller, more specialized classes. And even though college after college sounds like way too much school, here are some things to know about the kinds of degrees you can get if you go to graduate school, and what you can do with them.

- **Master's degree:** A master's degree is a degree you get with 1 or 2 more years of school after your BA or BS. It gives you more specialized knowledge about a certain topic, which you are tested on at the end of the program. Sometimes you write a big paper on your topic of study when you're done. Many people who are teachers have master's degrees in education—and other people in schools, such as social workers, guidance counselors, speech therapists and physical therapists probably have them, too.

- **Law school:** Law school is the graduate school you go to after you get your BA or BS degree if you want to become a lawyer or a judge. Many people who work in politics obtain this degree, too. Law school is typically 3 years, and lawyers and judges work in courts, but they also do a lot in offices.

- **PhD program:** Getting a PhD (or doctor of philosophy degree) involves doing research on a subject that has never been done before. This research can be on pretty much any subject you can think of, and these programs take anywhere from 3 to 7 years. For my PhD, I studied obsessive-compulsive disorder, which is a disorder where people focus on certain things and have a hard time breaking out of the cycle of focusing on those things. I worked with people with developmental delays and special needs. I studied for a long time to get my degree, and I learned how to be a teacher and how to do research, and I wrote a really long paper when I was done called a thesis—mine was over 300 pages! PhD students go on to be professors at universities or work for companies that need the specific knowledge they have. It is very exciting and rewarding to be a part of research that can change people's lives through the discoveries you might make. And you get to be called Doctor, too, which is kind of neat!

• **Medical school:** Medical school is the path to becoming a medical doctor, or "MD." Medical school takes 4 years, and after that, you typically spend more time to get specialized training for the area of medicine you plan to practice.

• **Dental school:** Dental school is similar to medical school in terms of how long it takes to finish, and in the end, you have a dental degree that lets you take care of people's teeth.

That's a lot to think about, I know. Although college and graduate school are not for everyone, it's good to get an idea of the variety of jobs and opportunities that are available to you if you choose that route.

NO COLLEGE?

Some people decide not to go to college at all, and that is also totally fine, depending on your interests and your desires. If you don't go to college after high school, what can you do? Well, some people go to trade schools to learn specific skills. Trade schools train you to have specialized jobs—like being an electrician, a plumber, a welder, a chef or even a makeup or hair stylist. When you go to a trade school, you can start as an apprentice until you have the skills to work on your own. You can start earning money sooner than if you went to college, but your job choices are going to be different.

Some people choose to join the military, often because the military pays for your education and you pay that debt back to the country in active service or in the reserves. Other people join the military because they feel it's their patriotic duty or because there's a long tradition in their family of being part of the military world. The decision to join the military is a huge one, and you should speak to your family if you are considering such a life-changing act. It is a brave and courageous decision to serve your country this way, but it is not without risks. You'll need your parents' permission if you decide to enlist before you turn 18, so make sure to open up a conversation as soon as you can to start thinking more about the impact it could have on you and your family.

◆ ◆ ◆

Causes

One of the most important ways to start thinking about how your life will look and how you can make your life matter for you and those you care about is to think about what you're passionate about. Finding a cause that is important to you helps you learn more about the world around you. Your brain needs a lot of information to form opinions about things, and the more you learn, the better you can know what you think and how to be a part of changing things in this world.

What matters to you? Are there things you hear about on the news that bother you? Maybe it's a story about racism or gun violence, or maybe news reports about the damage that is being done to the environment or to certain populations in the world. Maybe it's a story about how an animal was found in the street after it had been mistreated by its owners.

There are things you see going on right in your neighborhood that probably need your help. If you live in a city, there are concerns with how the homeless population is treated. There is litter in most every major city or town that needs to be dealt with. There are beaches that need cleaning up, parks that need repair and dozens of ways we need to make changes that will better things for everyone.

If you ever think about the problems in your community and our world and think it's just such a mess that it can never be fixed, guess what? You're wrong! There are lots of things we can do to make changes to this world, and every small gesture of loving kindness and care helps. You're not too young to think about ways you can give back to your community, your city, your country or even the world.

Even if a change is small, it can still be a big deal in the making. Here are some examples of charity projects that have been started by girls and young women not much older than you—and in some cases, maybe younger.

- **Alex's Lemonade Stand Foundation.** Alexandra "Alex" Scott was not even one year old when she was diagnosed with neuroblastoma, a type of cancer. When she was four years old,

she held her first cancer fund-raiser in her front yard and raised over $2,000. Tragically, she died when she was 8, but in her precious short life, she raised over $1 million for research into cures for childhood cancer. Her family has continued her legacy by continuing her mission, and Alex's Lemonade Stand has raised more than $120 million for cancer research and support for children with cancer and their families.

- **The Malala Fund.** Growing up in Pakistan in a home that encouraged education for girls but living in a culture that did not always support it, Malala Yousafzai began to write a blog at the age of 12 about the importance of education in her community. (See the box on page 63–64 for more on Malala.) At the age of 14, she won a prestigious award for her activism, and at 15, she was shot and injured by masked gunmen who wanted to stop her from continuing her work. She recovered and has become a spokesperson for the millions of girls who can't get an education because of social, economic, legal and political problems. She cofounded the Malala Fund to bring awareness to the importance of girls' education and to raise money and provide safe learning spaces to help empower girls to gain the confidence needed to demand further change.

- **Sole to Soul.** This organization started when the 3 Scott sisters (twins Hayleigh and Vienna, who were 13, and their 10-year-old sister, Sarah) heard in the news about a fire at a school in Kenya, Africa. They saw pictures of children at the school and noticed that all of the children were barefoot. They decided they wanted to raise money to send as many shoes to the children at this school as they could and they went door-to-door in their neighborhood collecting

secondhand shoes. They also set up donation spots
in their hometown and ended up raising $33,000 to
buy shoes for 1,500 children.

- **Positive Impact for Kids.** When she was 12,
  Leanne Joyce was at a cardiology checkup for a
  heart condition, and she was touched by a gift she
  was given by two teenagers who were hospital
  volunteers. Their act of kindness made her commit
  to giving back, and she formed an organization that
  helps fulfill the wish lists of hospitalized children in
  North Carolina and beyond. Over $25,000 has been
  raised, and that money is used to change children's
  lives in hospitals.

Although these organizations don't fix the entire problem of
pediatric cancer or give shoes to the millions of children all over
the world who still need them, and even though not every girl who
deserves an education will get one, these are examples of small and
significant projects that can have a tremendous impact on people.

You don't have to solve the whole problem at hand in order to
matter. You don't have to fix the world; you just have to start with
what you can do with your resources and build from there. Every
time you touch a person with kindness, the world gets a little bit
brighter. And you never know how your kindness will affect someone
else. It might cause a ripple effect so that your gesture makes them
want to do something about a problem, too—that's how this works.

Just like the girl who got a gift at her check-up and wanted to share it with others, you get to do your part and see how good it makes you feel to support a cause you believe in and to watch the positive effects you can help bring about. If establishing an organization or raising money door-to-door sounds like too much to start with, here are some examples of small things you can do that can have a big impact:

1. **Donate what you don't need.** Go through your closets and drawers and all of the closets and drawers in your house (with your parents' permission!) and find things you are not using anymore or that don't fit. You can donate used toys and clothes and really anything in fair condition to a local charity. Charities that run thrift stores sell items and use part of the profits to support the charity and the people who work there. There are also places to donate used clothing to homeless shelters in most major cities.

2. **Hold a clothing or food drive.** Any time you have the opportunity to interact with a group of people, such as at school or in after-school activities or community or religious activities, you have the opportunity to get a larger group of people to become involved in a charity project. When I was 15, I started a canned-food drive at the TV studio

where I was filming. I posted signs all over and walked around handing out flyers on my lunch break to anyone I could. My first year, I ended up raising an entire van full of canned goods for a homeless shelter. People loved the opportunity to contribute, and it felt especially good to be a part of something as a group. The more, the merrier!

3. **Collect spare change for a year.** Do you ever find loose change on the ground? Or have you ever put on a pair of pants you haven't worn in a while to find $1 or even $5 in the pocket that you had forgotten was there? I collect spare change and "found money" like that in a jar, and at the end of 12 months, I see how much is in there and donate it. Sometimes I pick a charity to send the money to, and sometimes I use that money to buy a sandwich and a drink for a homeless person sitting outside of a restaurant or store I'm going into. It's a small thing to do, but it does make a difference in someone's day, even in a small way.

4. **Pick up trash.** Whenever I go to a park or to the beach, I see trash everywhere, and I know you probably do, too. The next time you see trash, don't ignore it; pick it up and throw it out! Bring a plastic bag with you to the beach or the park or on a hike and collect trash. You can even use plastic

bags as "gloves" if you come across messy or sticky candy-bar wrappers and stuff like that. If everyone picked up a handful of trash, we wouldn't have so much trash lying around! It feels good to be a part of the solution and not the problem, and even though some places need a whole lot more cleanup than a few pieces of trash here and there, all you have to believe is that every little bit counts— because it does.

Volunteering

A terrific way to impact others is to take your passion for something and volunteer your time and energy toward it in a meaningful way. When you make a choice to volunteer for a cause you believe in, you are setting aside time to participate in working with an organization or group of people who want to make change in practical ways. In my life, I have volunteered to pack goodie boxes for soldiers overseas during the holidays, and I have helped answer phones and do office duties for organizations who could not afford to pay people to do that work. My favorite volunteer position when I was a teenager was working in a senior citizens' center.

How did that come about? Well, if you have any elderly people in your family or close circle of family friends, you might already know that spending time with someone who has seen a lot more of life than you have is a terrific way to learn about the world and how fast it's changing and will continue to change. I grew up with grandparents with very heavy accents who were immigrants from Eastern Europe. They left war-torn countries for the safety and security of America against all odds, working long hours in unsafe conditions to make money to support themselves and their families. They grew up in a world without computers or cell phones—can you imagine that?

I feel like you can get so much from being around seniors. So I literally walked into the office of a senior citizens' center in Hollywood when I was 17 and asked if I could volunteer there. The job I was given was to serve lunch to about 50 senior citizens every weekend.

The time I spent getting to know the people at this center was incredibly valuable. I made friends there, and I learned about how everyone came to Hollywood: some grew up there, and many of the people I served lunch to came to this country from other places: Cuba, Armenia, the Philippines. It was a real experience getting to know all of these different people and hearing about their lives. Many of them did not have much family, and I was sometimes the only person who wanted to talk to them. It made me feel good to be of service to them, and I could tell from their smiles and hugs that it made them feel good, too. A lot of my new friends spoke very slowly, and it helped me practice being patient and kind even if I had somewhere to go and things to do. I learned skills for preparing and serving food, and I found a source of compassion for these kind people that has stayed with me my whole life.

Volunteering gets you into the world of others and gives you the opportunity to make a difference in someone's life today.

Wrapping Up

Girling Up doesn't end when you become a legal adult; it's a journey that stays with you for the rest of your life, because it's about laying the foundation for a life of healthy and satisfying decisions. When we think about our lives as young women, there are so many ways we can make our lives matter. Planning for the future by identifying what you look for in a lifestyle and a career is important at your age, as is identifying ways you can start contributing to the world. Whether you become a stay-at-home mom or the president of the United States, there are ways you can make an impact on the people around you and the world around you. It starts by believing you matter and taking it one step at a time.

• AFTER THOUGHTS •

When I started planning *Girling Up*, I was certain that I had the scientific background to communicate what being female is like from a biological perspective; I knew enough about hormones and genetics and even psychology to tackle puberty and the physiological processes that take us from being a girl to being a woman. I knew enough about how the brain learns and incorporates information, and I was pretty sure I had enough heartache and love in my life to write about dating and romantic feelings and even sex. I knew I have ways I've learned to cope with difficult circumstances, and I have always been a person driven by a desire to make a positive impact on the world. So I was sure I could make that information accessible and even fun to read.

But what I wasn't sure about when I started writing this book was how it all would fit together—and even if it *should* fit together. What was the "big picture" here? Was I biting off more than I could chew? Should I just write a book about puberty? Or a book about coping with stress? Or maybe I should just write about my life and how I went from being a child actor to being a scientist?

I was worried that I wouldn't be able to make every single chapter part of a beautiful whole. Maybe it was too much. Could I really make ovaries and cramming for a physics test and liking boys no one else likes come together? Could I make the loss of my beloved cat fit somehow with my love for meditation and my knack for making necklaces? And do carbohydrates and volunteering at a homeless shelter even belong in the same book? What is this book *really* about? I started to doubt myself.

As I wrote, the reality of *Girling Up* came to me gradually. With every chapter, it became clearer and clearer. There is no way to talk about being a girl and becoming a woman—there is no way to tackle Girling Up—without including every aspect of us. Because we are not just a book on a shelf about a topic that has to be pieced together with a half dozen other books about other topics that are also us. We aren't just what we should be eating or who we are dating or what we are wearing or why we like science or don't. We are all of it.

We are our DNA, and we are the hormones that course through us. We are the vitamins and minerals we eat, and we are the fears and concerns we have about what we eat. We are the insecurities we have about not looking right and the things we do to try to feel right. We are the books we read and the ones we don't want to read, too. We are the love we feel when we hug our best friend, and we are the tears we cry when someone we love won't love us back. We are grief and sadness, and we are the things we do to try and make sense of a difficult world. We are the actions we take to change the things we see that are unjust, and we are as many possibilities as there are stars in the sky.

We are bodies that work, brains that learn, hearts that love, souls that struggle and women who matter. We are strong, smart and spectacular. We don't have to be superheroes to be all of the things we want to be. We just have to be us.

We are Girling Up in a world that may not always understand us, but the better we understand ourselves and the better we engage in the world as everything that we are made of and everything we make of ourselves and everything that we dream we can be, the better the chances are that we can make the impact we are destined to make.

Thank you for Girling Up with me.

◆ ACKNOWLEDGMENTS ◆

Thank you to my wonderful editor, Jill Santopolo, for reaching out to me and asking me to open up about my life and the way my brain works so that we could share it with an audience of young women. Jill, I so appreciate how you let me craft a comprehensive and ambitious treatise on what I see as the young female experience. You gave me such freedom to create a skeleton of a book much more daunting than I think you originally intended, and I thank you for being so enthusiastically on board and for talking me off many a *Girling Up* ledge. Thank you also for curbing my exclamation point enthusiasm! I am so proud of what we have done together and I hope we can positively impact so many people with this book!

I would like to thank my business reps Anthony Mattero (Foundry Media), my partner in crime, friend and manager, Tiffany Kuzon (Primary Wave), and Sarah Lerner (Katz Golden Rosenman LLP) for helping me navigate the business aspects of this book. A special modest fist bump goes to my mentor, friend and lawyer, Shep Rosenman, who also acts as spiritual therapist at times. Thank you to the sharpest tack in the box, Heather Weiss Besignano at E2W

Collective, for her publicity guidance and support from start to finish, as well as her cheerleading for everything we do 24/7, but especially for supporting the mission of empowering young women so enthusiastically.

Thank you especially to all of the assistants from my team who work so hard behind the scenes: Brandon Bonilla, Patricia Kennedy, Isabel Shanahan and Rebecca Malzahn. Talia Benamy in Jill's office gets a special thank-you with an exclamation point!

Thank you to Todd Malta, who managed all of the emails about this book and every other aspect of my life during its writing, as well as for editorial comments and suggestions based on being Quinn and Owen's dad.

In addition to our meticulous copy editor, Ana Deboo, I'd like to thank the powerhouse women who reviewed the book according to their fields of expertise; without them, the book would not have been as precise and carefully crafted as it is. These women are: neuroscientist Dr. Lisa Aziz-Zadeh, gynecologist Dr. Jessica Brown, registered dietician Rachel Goodman, pediatrician Dr. Lisa Nowell and school psychologist Dr. Samantha Winokur.

Everyone at Penguin has been so exceptional and I am particularly grateful to publisher Michael Green, Ellice Lee and Jenny Chung, who designed the book interior, and our endlessly patient book-jacket designers, Lindsey Andrews and Maria Fazio, who created a cover that truly reflects everything this book is. I have never had to make so few comments on any book in my life—all of the Penguin instincts have been 100 percent right on—and believe me, I try to find things to comment on! Thank you also to the marketing and PR teams at Penguin whose job it is to take this book to as many girls as we can. I appreciate this work we are doing together, and I am so grateful for your efforts on behalf of *Girling Up*.

Siobhán Gallagher's illustrations add so much to *Girling Up*, and I am so touched by the care she gave to creating images of a variety of girls in all shapes, sizes and colors. Thank you, Siobhán.

Thank you to my "junior" 11-year-old editors, Miles Roosevelt Bialik Stone and Iris Persephone Amos. Your input is very valuable, and I appreciate you being the first young people to read *Girling Up*.

Thank you to the cast, staff and crew of *The Big Bang Theory*. For the past 7 years, Stage 25 has been my home away from home, and I am so grateful to work among people who love what they do and do it so well. And a special punch in the belly to a kick-tuchus comedienne, friend, daughter, sister, wife and writer: Melissa Rauch, I could not have asked for a better person to have not want to share a dressing-room bathroom with me. You have gotten me through some very dark days and I thank you.

There are a few women from my early life I'd like to single out, who helped me become the woman I am today. Mrs. Ivy Cass, my elementary school English and calisthenics teacher, who taught me to spell like a fiend and run like a fierce athletic strong girl. Ms. Julie Drake, my elementary school drama teacher, fostered my love for positive creative attention as well as tremendous discipline in the form of theater. Dr. Firoozeh Rahbar, my biology tutor, who inspired my love for science in high school and helped catapult me into a life as a neuroscientist. And finally, Dr. Nancy Wayne, who would not let me submit my doctoral thesis until it was much much better than the first, second, third and fourth drafts that I gave her.

Rebbetzin Aviva Kohl and Allison "Jew in the City" Josephs taught me the ways of decorum, modesty and grace, and the ancient origins of these gifts have increased my concepts of my worth, dignity and the divine ability to love and be loved.

Thank you to my mother, who has braved the waters of raising a headstrong, oftentimes difficult, exceptionally unusual girl as her daughter. Mom: despite the fact that you never talked about most of the stuff in this book with me (which I will never let you live down), I am strong, smart and spectacular because of you. I know Dad ($z''l$) had something to do with it, too.

Thank you to the woman who raised two loving and gentle men, one of whom I created children with: Sherrie Stone, you are a constant source of womanly inspiration to me. Thank you.

To my cousin, Rebekah Goldstein: our years growing up together—me 6 years ahead of you—taught me so much; sometimes it was unclear who was more experienced and mature! Thank you for being my ally through so many of life's ups and downs. You're the best SWOTS ever.

Thank you to the women I have learned to let in to my life after years of fearing the closeness of women, who have helped me complete the daunting task of continuing to Girl Up. These beautiful, fierce, intelligent, loving women are Kari "Pitzy" Druyen, Nancy Stringer and my buddy Elsa Rodarte.

To Immanuel Shalev, thank you for your friendship, your belief in me and your full-time career as my guardian angel. I could not have done most of the past 5 years of this life without you by my side and in my head. I am blessed to have you.

The women who have powered my most complicated *Girling Up* journey are Dr. Nancy Vanderheide and Shawn Crane; thank you for helping me become the woman God intended me to be. I am grateful for you every day.

Thank you, Robert Mathes, for being with me always, but especially as I wrote this book and navigated our life together as it unfolded. You have helped me define emotional intimacy very clearly not only for this book, but for our journey as well. Thank you.

Thank you to the father of my children, Michael Stone, for your flexibility as I careen through life and try to do right for our boys. I appreciate the time you give me to write and work and to handle all of the curveballs I get thrown. You are a wonderful and devoted father and our sons are infinitely lucky to have you.

Finally, to my boys, Miles and Frederick: thank you for being so understanding with me as I worked on this book, and for not being understanding sometimes as well; since it was at those times that you reminded me to live in this world with you, and not only to live in my work. I hope you encounter many strong, smart, spectacular people in your lives and that you do great things with them by your side. I am so blessed that you came over the Rainbow Bridge to find me. I love you more than sushi.

• INDEX •

NOTE: Page numbers in *italics* indicate illustrations.